PLAYBACK

A GUIDE TO REVIEWING ACTIVITIES

Published 1993 by:
The Duke of Edinburgh's Award,
Gulliver House, Madeira Walk, Windsor, Berkshire SL4 1EU
in association with
Endeavour Scotland

Distributed by:
The Award Scheme Ltd.,
69, Dublin Street, Edinburgh EH3 6NS

Designed and illustrated by David Hilditch,
Ard Bruach, Lochearnhead, Scotland.

Printed by Callander Printers, Callander, Scotland.

British Library Cataloguing-in-Publication Data.
A catalogue record for this book is available from the British Library.

ISBN 0 905425 09 X
Playback: A Guide to Reviewing Activities. (pbk)

Funded by:
The Special Projects Group of
The Duke of Edinburgh's Award
Endeavour Scotland
The Trustee Savings Bank
The Bank of Scotland

PLAYBACK

A GUIDE TO REVIEWING ACTIVITIES

ROGER GREENAWAY

THE DUKE OF EDINBURGH'S AWARD
Published in association with
Endeavour Scotland

CONTENTS

I hear ... I forget

I see ... I remember

I do + REVIEW **... I learn**

Confucius, Chinese Philosopher 551 - 479 BC

PREFACE

PLAYBACK is for anyone who uses activities in their work with young people. It is a practical handbook about learning from experience. It describes how to review activities in ways which stimulate and support personal and social development.

The methods and skills described in these pages can be applied to the reviewing of *any* activity: adventures, exercises, expeditions, experiments, games, simulations, sports, service, skills, residential experience, work experience, etc.

It is a collection of reviewing techniques for use by anyone who uses activities as a means to an end. This includes: counsellors, instructors, assessors, leaders, social workers, teachers, trainers, tutors, and youth workers (all of whom are referred to in these pages as 'reviewers'). The techniques, although particularly appropriate for groupwork, can be adapted to work with individual young people.

PLAYBACK is designed to serve both as an introduction to reviewing, and as a source of ideas and insights for more experienced 'reviewers'. The methods described in this book have been chosen with these considerations in mind:

- Most do not require specialist skills.
- Most are relevant to work with people of all ages.
- The techniques represent a wide spectrum of reviewing styles (active, creative and discussion-based).
- All techniques can be readily adapted and developed to suit different situations.

The best qualification for using this handbook is a willingness to try something new: a personal commitment to learning from experience.

1 INTRODUCING REVIEWING

I used to interrogate my children when I collected them from school. It would go something like this ...

What did you do today? (nothing) Did you do reading today? (no) Did you learn anything new today? (no) Were you good today? (yes) Was there anything special about today? (not really) What was the best thing about today? (all of it)

The more questions I asked, the more I seemed to be shutting the door on any discussion about their day at school.

Now when I collect my children from school I use sign language! I start by asking them "What sort of day was it?". They respond with thumbs up or thumbs down, or (more usually) one thumb up and one thumb down. I then say to one of them, "Which do you want to tell me about first?". Sometimes they will choose to tell me the good news first, sometimes the bad. Sometimes they will have so much news that they will 'borrow' extra thumbs. More often than not, this quickly leads into an interesting conversation about their day at school.

'Thumbs up or down?' won't work for long, but it works well just now.

I was simply an interested parent trying to communicate with my children, trying to encourage them to tell me something (anything!) about their day. I was trying to open up communication about a recent experience.

This example of an all too familiar situation now serves to introduce some basic points about reviewing ...

COMMUNICATING: Reviewing involves communicating about recent experience. Once the lines of communication are open, the reviewing process can be developed in many different ways. It does not necessarily involve special techniques, but techniques are very useful when 'ordinary' ways of communicating are not working well.

QUESTIONING SKILLS: There is much more to reviewing than asking the right questions, but good questioning skills are very useful. For example, open questions ('What..?', 'How..?', 'Why..?') generally produce more informative responses than closed ones which prompt 'yes' or 'no' answers.

NON-VERBAL TECHNIQUES: Non-verbal means of expression (even as simple as 'thumbs up or down?'), can provide useful 'starters' for initiating reviews. Non-verbal techniques can also provide useful ways of communicating at deeper levels.

INNOVATION: Most reviewing techniques seem to have a limited 'shelf life'. A certain amount of routine is useful, but new techniques capture the imagination and remotivate learners, as well as opening up new ways of seeing, communicating and learning. It pays to be innovative!

YOUNG PEOPLE'S CREATIVITY: Young people frequently have good ideas about how to review a particular activity. Some reviewing techniques might need to follow set procedures, but others can also be readily devised or improvised by young people themselves, once they have a basic understanding of what reviewing is about.

the scope of reviewing

- Bethan describes the wonderful moment when she found the courage to vault over the box - she felt she could conquer the world.
- Individuals walk out to their 'magic spots' and write down what they want to remember.
- Mary quietly explains the significance of the relationship she established with an elderly lady at the hospice.
- Young people 'with low concentration spans' stay up long after midnight talking about their experiences.
- Majid eventually believes the good things that others are saying about him.
- Charlie tries to express the sheer elation of playing his saxophone for the first time to an audience - knowing they wanted more.
- Martina slowly tells her story about the discrimination she faces as a disabled young woman.
- The group scapegoat paints a picture of his recent experiences and shows it to the group.
- Errol bravely explains how the police service course helped him to come to terms with his rebellious attitude towards authority.
- A split group re-enacts incidents which created the split during the expedition, and starts to build bridges.
- Young people celebrate a rare success with a song.

These are all real examples of young people expressing what they experience, and learning through doing so. These also happen to be examples of individuals (or groups) making significant breakthroughs in their development. They are examples which challenge some common assumptions about reviewing ...

"Reviewing is analysing mistakes.": It can also involve unravelling puzzling experiences, reliving enjoyable ones, or investigating the causes of success.

"Reviewing is all talk.": Reviewing does not need to be 'all talk' - there are many other ways of communicating effectively.

"Reviewing ends with looking ahead.": It is not always necessary to finish with planning - some benefits happen without the aid of a plan or action point.

What matters in reviewing, however formal or informal, routine or adventurous it might be, is that it actually helps people to learn from their experience.

Reviewing methods cover a wide spectrum. Reviewing can take the form of private reflection, with individuals quietly thinking or writing about an experience: in the right circumstances (and there are many ways of setting it up) private reflection can be a highly rewarding form of reviewing. Reviewing can equally be a dynamic interpersonal experience - to the extent that it can even be *more* of an experience than the event being reviewed. This may seem a strange idea, because it is often assumed that the 'doing' part of a learning cycle is the dynamic stage, with the 'review' being seen as a relatively tame experience.

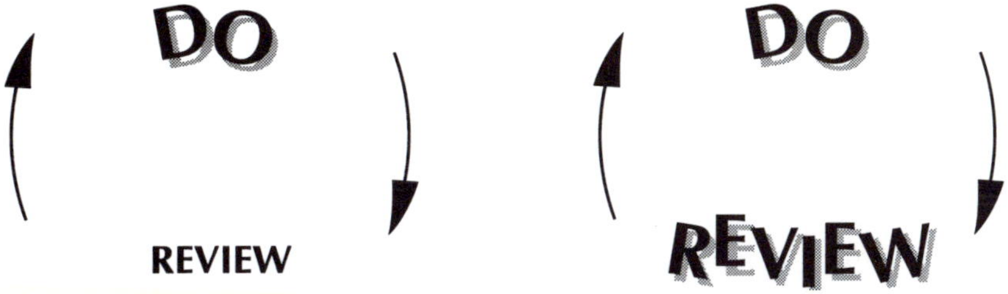

Young people enjoy reviewing which meets their development needs and will often pick it out as being the highlight of an activity-based programme. Young people who have not responded well to other forms of learning are often found to be amongst the keenest participants in reviewing sessions.

> *"At the end of each project we had the reviews and to me these were the best things we did, because we learnt a hell of a lot about each other and how we did during the project. We spoke our thoughts, expressed our opinions and ideas throughout the group, and so built our relationships up even higher. I think we were trusted more as well. This came about because we had proven we are grown-ups and will help one another if trouble arises. It was a brilliant week which all of us enjoyed."* [1]

experience plus reflection equals learning [2]

> *"Even high quality experiences do not result in learning unless complemented by equally high quality reflection."* [3]
>
> *"Experience in itself is neither productive nor unproductive, it is how you reflect on it that makes it significant or not significant for good or ill ..."* [4]

Theories of experiential learning are generally presented in the form of learning cycles which divide reviewing (or 'reflection') into two or more stages. These cycles are a useful guide to the reviewer because they provide a sequence which can be followed. The first example of an experiential learning cycle shown below is chosen because it is a synthesis of several other learning models (one of the best known of which is shown on the right).

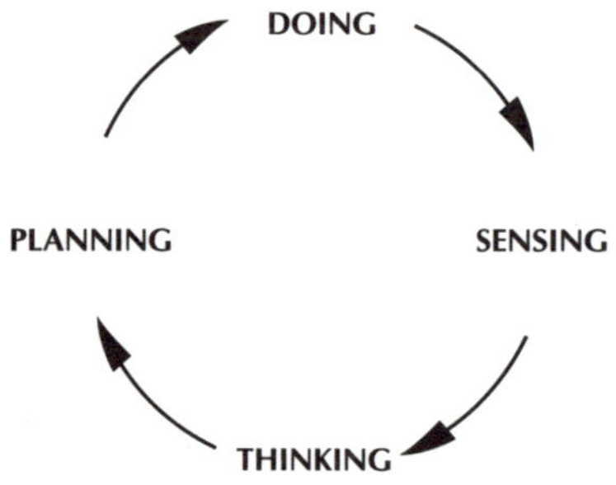

Juch [5] (1983)

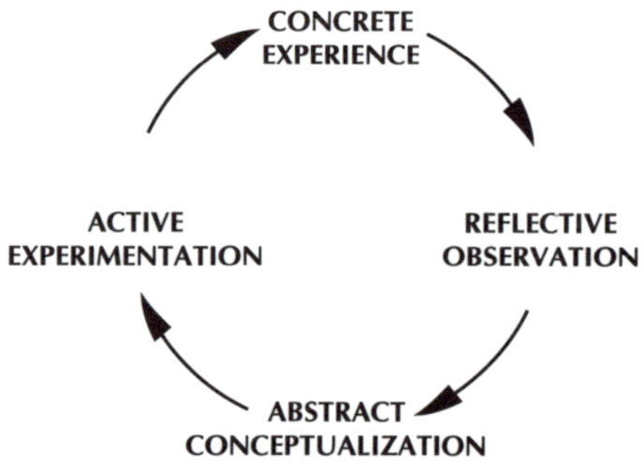

Kolb and Fry [6] (1975)

Experiential learning cycles

One of the main values of thinking in terms of a cycle or sequence is that it discourages reviewers from taking unproductive short cuts. Inexperienced reviewers tend to be in a rush to identify what people have learned, without providing sufficient opportunity for much learning to happen. The reviewing sequence described next shows one way in which the above learning models can be interpreted and applied in practice. It is also used on page 29 as a means of indexing the methods listed in Chapter 3.

a four stage reviewing sequence [7]

1: EXPERIENCE The first stage is to establish, 'play back', or 'relive' what happened. This stage can serve as a useful reminder of significant incidents. It can help to set the agenda for later stages, but the main focus of this first stage is on *what happened.*

2: EXPRESS The second stage is a vital one, but tends to be the stage most at risk if review time is limited. It recognises that activities (especially new or challenging ones) stimulate the senses and arouse emotions. This stage focuses on the *quality* of the experience: "What was it like?", "How did it feel?"

3: EXAMINE The third stage is more analytical and rational. 'All-talk' reviews tend to arrive too soon at this stage, especially if reviewers are too impatient to draw out the learning from the activity. If it has been a 'whole person' experience, it is important to use review methods which match the fullness of the experience.

4: EXPLORE The fourth stage is the most practical stage. It involves preparing to try out something that has been prompted by earlier stages of the sequence. It would usually involve setting targets. Above all, it is important to keep the sense of curiosity and exploration alive.

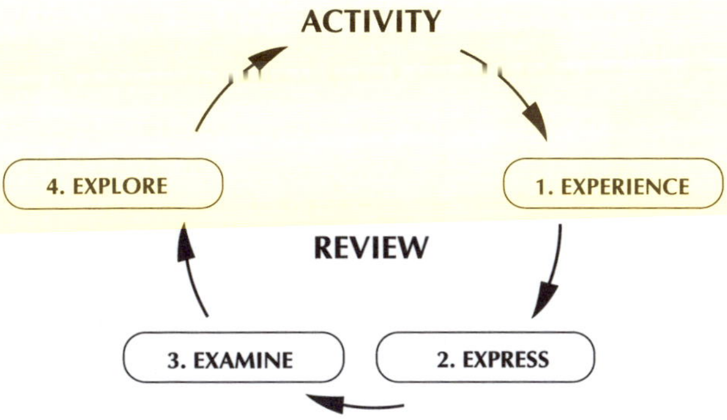

how much reviewing?

Models and sequences are useful guides, but there are always exceptions. A quick 'one stage' review is better than none at all. Some reviewing will often take place naturally during the activity itself, so it is worth finding out how much informal reviewing has happened, and building on that. In some activities, it may seem that little has happened that is worth reviewing. If this is the case, the main question will be about how to set up a more eventful activity that will be worth reviewing. At other times, it might seem that an activity has been so 'worthwhile' that there is little that a review could add. Occasionally, perhaps - but success should not be wasted! 'Worthwhile' experiences create ideal opportunities for understanding how success happened, for exchanging positive feedback, and for finding ways of building on success.

If activities are left unreviewed too often, the *status quo* (however 'good' or 'bad' that might be) is left undisturbed, and change, learning or development is less likely to happen. Without regular reviewing of activities, groups are more likely get stuck at one particular stage of development, and it then becomes increasingly difficult to create a group climate which supports learning. Without regular reviewing there is a risk that individuals will also get stuck, with activities tending to re-inforce fixed patterns of behaviour and fixed views of self and others.

Reviewing can be applied to both pleasant and unpleasant experiences. If the experience was a negative one for some or all participants, reviewing can help to minimise negatives and accentuate positives. In many situations it is important to examine the negative aspects and to provide opportunities for understanding and mutual support. But if reviewing is applied *exclusively* to negative experiences, there is a danger that reviewing will itself become a negative experience and will simply be seen as a means of prolonging the agony!

terminology

'REVIEWING' AND 'EVALUATION'
There is considerable overlap in the everyday usage of 'reviewing' and 'evaluation', but in activity-based learning it is helpful to distinguish between them in this way:
- the main purpose of 'reviewing' is to *increase* value;
- the main purpose of 'evaluation' is to *judge* value.

Asking for a judgment *immediately* after an activity, would be like asking for the final score at half time. If the activity is equivalent to the 'first half', then a good review in the 'second half' should improve the scoreline. 'Evaluation' typically looks at the outcomes from the whole learning process rather than from half-way through the learning process (before the review has taken place).

EXPERIENCE ➔	REVIEW ➔	EVALUATION	
✔	✘	✘	guessing what people experience
✔	✘	✔	finding out what people experience
✔	✔	✘	helping people to learn from experience
✔	✔	✔	helping people to learn, plus evaluating the whole process

If young people are accustomed to 'reviewing', the process of 'evaluation' will be much easier, because young people will be more able to express themselves and to provide evidence of their learning and development.

a definition of reviewing

Reviewing is an activity that is used to encourage people to reflect, describe, analyse and communicate what they have recently experienced. [8] It is any process in which the purpose or effect is to enhance the value of a recent experience. It can involve focusing attention on the past, present or future. Alternative terms for 'reviewing' are: 'processing', 'debriefing' and 'reflection'.

The term 'reviewing', as used in this book, operates at two levels:

- First, it applies to the process of learning from experience itself (which can, for example, take the form of private reflection).
- Secondly, it applies to the process of facilitating learning from experience for others, as in:

> *"I want to improve my reviewing skills for working with young people."*

Say this aloud and read on!

---

notes and references

1 Manpower Services Commission (1984). *Residential Training in the Youth Training Scheme*, MSC, Sheffield.

2 Experiential learning predates institutionalised forms of learning by several thousand years. John Dewey's simple formula has inspired many others to rediscover this forgotten art. Dewey, J. (1938) *Experience and Education*, New York, Collier Books.

3 Teschner, D.P. and Wolter, J. (1990). *Beyond Minimum Competencies...* in Miles, J.C. and Priest, S., Editors. *Adventure Education*, Venture Publishing Inc., State College, PA.

4 Bolton, G. (1979). *Towards a Theory of Drama in Education*, Longman

5 This model incorporates models about how young people and managers learn: experiential learning is for all ages. Juch, B. (1983). *Personal Development Theory and Practice in Management Training*. Shell International/Wiley.

6 Kolb, D. and Fry, R. (1975) *Towards an Applied Theory of Experiential Learning* in Cooper, C., Editor. *Theories of Group Processes.* New York, Wiley.

7 Greenaway, R. (1992). *Reviewing by Doing* in Loynes, C. Editor *The Journal of Adventure Education and Outdoor Leadership.* 9(2), 21-25.

8 The first sentence of this definition comes from: Quinsland, L.K. and Van Ginkel, A. (1984). How to Process Experience in *The Journal of Experiential Education*, 7(2), 8-13, Association for Experiential Education, Boulder, Colorado.

2 PURPOSES

a sense of purpose

I once worked on a residential training course for football apprentices in which the main purpose was 'teamwork'. Four professional football clubs sent teams of apprentices to take part in a variety of teamwork activities (without a football). The purpose of the course was very clear, as was the thinking behind it:

football skills + teamwork skills = a successful football team

The absence of footballs made it easier to concentrate on the main purpose of the course: 'teamwork' was the subject of every review.

Different readers will have different kinds of purpose in mind for reviewing. You may have a single straightforward purpose, as in the example above. You may have broad developmental aims in mind that change and evolve. You may find that you start out with narrow objectives which broaden out. You may start with a general aim within which you negotiate short term goals. You may have a list of aims so long that anything you do will 'fit' several aims at once! Or your objective may be to help young people to clarify *their own* objectives, and to offer support if and when needed.

Reviewing has a place in all of these styles of work. Wherever there is a *sense of purpose* related to an activity, reviewing can help to clarify it and achieve it. The next two pages on 'finding a purpose' apply to *any* kind of purpose underlying an activity, such as:

- to provide enjoyable experiences which encourage participation;
- to demonstrate or practise what has already been learned;
- to assess learning and development needs;
- to meet learning and development needs;
- to discover previously unknown capabilities.

finding a purpose

The purpose of a *review* can be exactly the same as that of the *activity*. For example, the main purpose of an activity might be 'to develop communication skills', 'to encourage co-operation', 'to improve performance', or simply 'to try the activity to see if you like it'. Whatever the purpose, it can be followed up in a review:

PURPOSE → ACTIVITY → REVIEW → OUTCOME

If anything is preventing the main purpose from being achieved, then reviewing can be used for 'troubleshooting' side issues along the way:

PURPOSE → ACTIVITY → REVIEW → OUTCOME
↓ ↑
REVIEW

There is rarely just one purpose. It often happens that activities are multi-purpose, or that a group (or individual) is working on a number of different aims or issues at the same time. In these situations, it is useful to single out one particular purpose as a focus for review. The first stage of the review would be to choose a priority subject from this 'standing agenda' of purposes. One way of doing this is to ask participants to identify what they saw as being the main issues or achievements during the activity:

SEVERAL PURPOSES → ACTIVITY → ONE PURPOSE → REVIEW → OUTCOME

Sometimes it is necessary to create a new purpose at the start of a review. Perhaps the activity is the primary source of motivation, and participants are only vaguely aware of the wider purposes that are in the mind of the 'reviewer'. In these circumstances the priority is to introduce a clear purpose onto the reviewing agenda. When first introducing reviewing, it is useful to keep to subjects or purposes which clearly add to the enjoyment of activities (while also extending participants' interests and abilities into new areas):

VAGUE PURPOSE → ACTIVITY → CLEAR PURPOSE → REVIEW → OUTCOME

When there is a clear purpose that is understood and supported by young people, they will readily put energy and commitment into the learning process. A clear, shared purpose helps to energise the learning process, but the learning process itself always brings 'extra' benefits - whatever the main purpose might be. Some of these 'extra benefits' are circled in the diagram below.

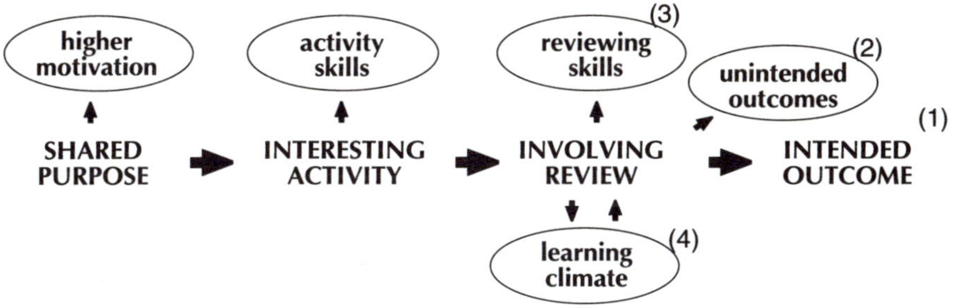

The above diagram also shows four types of outcome which result from reviewing activities:

1) the intended outcome - in line with the initial purpose;

2) unintended outcomes - which result from reviewing whatever actually happened (also known as 'serendipitous' learning);

3) acquiring reviewing skills - learning to learn from experience;

4) a favourable learning climate - for achieving outcomes 1, 2 and 3.

A shared purpose and an interesting activity help to create a climate for reviewing, but participants may not always be in the best frame of mind for reviewing, and the group may not happen to provide an 'ideal learning climate'. This means that, in practice, most reviewing methods will have a dual purpose: both to create a climate which supports learning and development (which is considered next); and to process experiences in ways that produce useful outcomes (two pages on).

improving the learning climate

Learning and development are more likely to happen if the learning climate is responsive to individuals' developmental needs. A number of developmental needs [1] are listed here, together with brief examples of how reviewing can help to meet them.

BELONGING: finding out how much each individual felt a part of the group during the activity, and then discussing what the group and individuals can do to increase everyone's sense of belonging to it.

ACCEPTANCE: encouraging respect for individuals and for expression of individuality; finding the situations and methods through which each individual can readily communicate and express themselves.

CARE AND FRIENDSHIP: encouraging group members to notice and appreciate care and friendship during activities. This can be encouraged by rounds of appreciation ("I appreciated it when you ...")

PRAISE AND RECOGNITION: analysing group achievements in terms of who contributed what, and tracing back causal links. A round starting "I felt ignored/unnoticed when ..." invites recognition from others.

RESPONSIBILITY: asking individuals about what responsibilities they had during an activity, what they found easy or difficult, and what kind and level of responsibility they would like next time.

SELF-RESPECT: asking participants to make positive statements about themselves: "My ten best points during the activity were ...". Positive, honest appraisal from the group will also add to self-respect.

CREATIVITY: asking a group to list all the ideas that came up during the activity, using creative reviewing techniques, encouraging young people to take part in devising activities and designing programmes.

ACHIEVEMENT: celebrating achievements by repeating them, publicising them, recreating them through art, or re-enacting them through drama. Making a chart which illustrates their route to achievement.

NEW EXPERIENCES: asking what was new, strange or different about the experience being reviewed; providing new experiences during the review itself by using a stimulating variety of reviewing methods.

By reviewing activities we show that we *care* about what young people experience; that we *value* what they have to say; and that we are interested in the *progress* of each individual's learning and development. But it should not just be the reviewer who demonstrates these attitudes: ideally the whole group should reflect them - especially if it is an influential peer group. Even with 'difficult' groups (which are resistant to change and learning), it is the reviewing process itself which provides one of the key strategies for influencing the group climate. Two examples are provided on this page; many more are found in the next chapter.

- A few basic 'GROUND RULES' (the minimum necessary), negotiated with the group, and expressed in positive statements, can help to gain commitment to behaviour that supports learning. The rules are created by reviewing the initial experiences of the group, for example, by completing some of the following sentence beginnings in paired interviews, and then discussing responses as a whole group:

  What's good about the atmosphere in this group is ... It is difficult to speak up in this group when ... This group is good/not good at ... I would be happier in this group if ... I would take part more in reviews/activities if ... I would learn/benefit more if ...

- 'MIXING THE GROUP' (as much as possible) helps to change patterns of relationships within a group. Some people prefer the relative intimacy of reviewing in pairs or sub-groups; others prefer larger groups - so it pays to change group sizes frequently. It is also important to keep changing pairings or subgroups, so that everyone gets to work with everyone else, as this helps to prevent cliques forming. If young people are being asked to work with partners they don't get on with ('unlikely pairs'), it is particularly important to provide them with a reviewing task which they are likely to achieve and enjoy. Ask everyone to report back to the whole group on how they got on with each other. If the answer is at least as good as "better than expected", then the strategy is working.

processing the experience

Five reviewing processes which facilitate learning and development:

RE-VIEWING THE EXPERIENCE
Reviewing provides a means of seeing an experience from new points of view - literally 're-viewing' the experience. These new perspectives might include appreciating what it's like to be in someone else's shoes, or recognising that there could be more than one explanation of what happened. Some reviewing methods 'zoom out', revealing the bigger picture, while others 'zoom in', placing a single incident under the spotlight. Where views are fixed, reviewing can unfix them, revealing a world where alternatives, ambiguities and different shades of meaning exist. Where views are chaotic and incoherent, reviewing can reveal meaningful patterns.

ADDING VALUE TO THE EXPERIENCE
The habit of reviewing increases perceptiveness *during* experiences. Knowing that there is a review coming up, participants tend to anticipate potential review issues during the activity itself. Reviewing can encourage learners to be both more inward and more outward looking - noticing more about themselves, others, and their surroundings. Increased awareness enriches their experiences, and by valuing their own experiences more, young people will also be valuing themselves more.

MAKING SENSE OF THE EXPERIENCE
Simply providing the opportunity for talking things through and for being listened to can help a young person to make sense of their experience. If the experience has been a confusing or unpleasant one, a sensitive and enlightening review can help young people to work through their disappointments in a constructive way. If a person's low self-esteem provides a barrier to learning, then a supportive review can help positive messages to get through. If young people experience failure or success, the causes can be analysed so that they learn how to avoid failure and how to achieve success.

MAKING CONNECTIONS WITH OTHER EXPERIENCES

Reviewing enables people to link their learning across different activities, and to make connections with everyday life.

The connections may happen as the result of a plan to apply what was learned; or connections may happen retrospectively, when something triggers a young person's memory of a previous learning experience. Sometimes a conscious 'trigger' is not needed because the learning has become internalised, and has become an integral part of that person's make-up. Sometimes the benefits will be transferred at an entirely different level of learning - when young people apply their improved *learning* abilities in new situations.

DEVELOPING LEARNING SKILLS

Reviewing enhances young people's ability to learn from individual or group experiences. As their ability to learn from experience develops, they become more able to take responsibility for their own learning and development. Improved learning ability, together with increased confidence, allows young people to become more independent, more capable of self-development, and more aware of the ways in which others can help (or hinder) their learning. The ability to learn from experience is a powerful asset which creates opportunities for further learning, development and empowerment.

> *"The ultimate aim of reviewing exercises is to make reviewing a habit, thus stimulating and developing people's ability to learn from experience."* [2]

---

notes and references

1 This list of needs is drawn from the work of Maslow (1954), Lindgren (1956) and Kellmer-Pringle (1965). Similar needs have also been identified by Carl Rogers (1969) as being the critical needs to satisfy in order to create the "freedom to learn".

2 John Hunt and Penny Hitchin in *Creative Reviewing*, 2nd edition (1989), Groundwork, Grange-over-Sands, Cumbria.

3 METHODS

"It was really good. I learnt how to work in a group and although I wasn't used to it I found out it was much easier. I hardly used to go to school and now I've left. I've always been scared to move with other people in a crowd, but at Brathay I found it much easier to listen to other views, to challenge someone else and to do something. I felt like I was at home. I was welcomed - they were kind. They would like to know your problems and try to help you solve them. We were eating together, drinking together, and doing activities together like it was my family." [1]

"The discussions were an important part of the day because they helped me to put in perspective all the things we were learning." [2]

making a start: a basic toolkit

If you are selling the idea of reviewing to a group, or experimenting with reviewing for the first time, these eight methods will provide a useful and dependable variety from which to choose.

1) **ROUNDS**: useful for many purposes, and for introducing some basic principles about reviewing in groups. (p 90)

2) **MID-ACTIVITY REVIEWING**: the easiest way of selling reviewing, especially if making use of a break during an activity in which young people are having difficulties, and want to succeed. (p 60)

3) **UPS AND DOWNS**: perhaps the easiest and most interesting way of encouraging awareness of others and the expression of feelings. Variations include a 'one minute' version or a 'one hour' version. (p 106)

4) **PICTURES**: a way of creating many talking points and opportunities for informal one-to-one reviewing; they can stimulate more perceptive discussion than even the most skilled questioning. (p 68)

5) **POSITIONS**: a method which quickly allows everyone to make their 'positions' clear on a particular issue, and increases participation in discussions. (p 72)

6) **DISCUSSION**: 'remedial' methods for tackling one of the most common problems in group discussions: dominance by a few individuals and little participation by others. (p 40)

7) **SCORES**: methods which recognise that it is quicker to think of a number than to construct a sentence. Scores help to speed up the reviewing process, and quickly highlight the subjects or issues most worth talking about. (p 92)

8) **PREDICTIONS**: a way to exploit everyone's betting instincts. Their degree of accuracy generates useful talking points for reviewing. (p 74)

some practical considerations

Thinking ahead obviously increases the chances of successful reviewing, but it is always better to have an unplanned/improvised review than to have no review at all. The questions below should not deter you from reviewing: for readers in an optimistic frame of mind these questions will remind you of opportunities for reviewing that you may have overlooked. Most of these questions are considered in more detail on other pages and can be found by referring to key words in the main index on page 139.

OVERALL STRATEGY
What kind of review would meet the needs of the young people?
What preparation would help to produce this kind of review?
What kind of experience would lead into this kind of review?
What kind of activity would create this kind of experience?

PURPOSE
When and how are group aims and objectives decided?
When and how are individual aims and objectives decided?

TIMING
Immediately after the event? After a short break? Next week?
A quick on-the-spot review, followed by a longer one later?
After another activity, reviewing both together?
Same duration as the activity? Or shorter? Or longer?

PLACE
Where the activity took place? (while experiences are fresh and are the natural topic of conversation, and while it is easier to demonstrate a point or repeat parts of the activity)
While walking, travelling or eating? (providing a chance for informal reviewing, especially with 'loud' or 'quiet' individuals who find it difficult to participate in a group setting)
The review room? (Ideal surroundings? Comfortable? Air-conditioned? Quiet? No interruption or distraction? Plenty of space and resources?)

CLIMATE
How structured? How informal? Easygoing? Businesslike? Free-flowing? Challenging? Fun?
Covering lots of ground quickly or one aspect in depth?
Using several reviewing methods or just one?

GROUND RULES
No contract or agreement unless problems arise?
Rules expressed positively? (more do's than don'ts)
Agreeing principles rather than rules? (more respect for principles?)
What is negotiable? What is not negotiable?

PARTICIPATION
How will you maintain high levels of involvement for each individual?
How will you help those who cannot express themselves readily? (especially as they may have the greatest need to do so)

ENDING
How will you decide when to finish? Will this be agreed in advance?
Will important points be summarised? How?
How will you gauge and attend to emotional needs at the end?
How will you help learners to work out realistic follow-up action?
How will learners be supported in carrying out follow-up action?

THE ROLE AND STYLE OF REVIEWER
Provided that you are consistent and sincere in your general attitude and values, variations in your role and style will allow and encourage young people to try out different roles and styles themselves. The reviewer's role and style can vary considerably according to which methods are chosen.

EMPOWERING YOUNG PEOPLE
Remember that you are helping young people to learn from their experience. Encourage young people to develop reviewing skills as well as activity skills. Listen to young people's ideas and you, and they, will have many more methods from which to choose.

index of reviewing methods (page headings)

The main index at the back of the book lists over a hundred reviewing methods. Only the forty page headings for reviewing methods are listed here. They are indexed in three ways:

1) in alphabetical order: their actual order in the book.
2) in relation to the four stages of reviewing.
3) in relation to five styles of reviewing.

FOUR STAGES OF REVIEWING

Reviewing is likely to be more effective if it follows a planned sequence. If readers are accustomed to thinking in terms of one particular experiential learning cycle, they are likely to find that it follows a similar sequence to the one summarised below (first described on page 13).

STAGE 1: EXPERIENCE - facts - the facts of the experience;
STAGE 2: EXPRESS - feelings - the quality of the experience;
STAGE 3: EXAMINE - findings - issues, questions, analysis, feedback;
STAGE 4: EXPLORE - futures - setting targets, preparing, trying out.

The numbers opposite (under the heading 'REVIEW STAGE') indicate the stages for which the methods are most useful.

FIVE STYLES OF REVIEWING

The five (overlapping) categories listed below give an indication of the main style of reviewing in each double page section. For example, a reviewer interested in using 'creative' methods can quickly find seven methods indexed in this way on the opposite page. As readers get to know the book they will also discover creative methods within other sections, because many of the reviewing methods described are a mixture of these five styles:

ACTIVE: drama-based and/or physical;
CREATIVE: visual, expressive arts;
FEEDBACK: giving and receiving feedback;
VERBAL: varieties of group discussion;
INDIVIDUAL: a mainly individual focus.

PLUS, MINUS and INTERESTING

The symbols ▲ ▼ ◆ are used to highlight:
plus points (▲),
minus points (▼),
interesting points (◆).

	PAGE TITLE	REVIEW STAGE				MAIN STYLE
30	action points				4	individual
32	action replay	1				active
34	arts		2			creative
36	cards			3		feedback
38	cartoons	1		3		creative
40	discussion			3	4	verbal
42	evaluation	1	2	3	4	verbal
44	forces			3	4	verbal
46	gifts		2	3		feedback
48	guided reflection	1	2	3	4	individual
50	human sculptures	1	2	3	4	active
52	independent reviewing			3	4	verbal
54	labelling			3	4	active
56	learning to learn				4	individual
58	metaphors		2			creative
60	mid-activity reviewing	1	2	3	4	verbal
62	objectives	1		3	4	individual
64	observing	1		3		feedback
66	performing	1	2	3	4	active
68	pictures	1	2	3	4	creative
70	playback	1	2	3	4	verbal
72	positions	1		3		active
74	prediction	1		3	4	feedback
76	preparation			3		verbal
78	presentations	1	2	3	4	creative
80	questionnaires	1		3		individual
82	questions	1	2	3	4	verbal
84	repeating the activity				4	active
86	reports	1	2	3	4	individual
88	roles	1		3		verbal
90	rounds	1	2	3	4	verbal
92	scores	1		3	4	individual
94	self-images	1	2	3	4	creative
96	sketch map	1	2	3	4	creative
98	soundtrack				4	individual
100	speaking for a partner	1	2	3		feedback
102	stories	1	2	3	4	verbal
104	tape-recording	1	2			verbal
106	ups and downs	1	2			individual
108	video	1	2	3	4	feedback
110	reviewing to develop responsibility: a sequence of methods					
111	reviewing to develop co-operation: a sequence of methods					

ACTION POINTS are objectives which originate from the activity being reviewed. They provide a means of carrying forward what is learned from one activity to the next, or to a similar situation.

An action point is a specific and achievable short term goal. It may be one small step towards a larger goal, based on the belief that it will make the next step easier and will generate momentum.

The review methods described here are methods which help to *produce* action points. If the four stage reviewing sequence described in Chapter 1 is being followed, then it is during the fourth and final stage of this process that ideas for action points will be collected from previous stages and converted into clear statements of intended action.

TANDEM REVIEWING

In a programme or sequence of activities, whatever is learned from one activity can often be readily applied to the next activity in the form of an action point. A much bigger conceptual leap is needed (and much more determination) to apply what is learned to a different situation, in a different place, and with different people.

> One of the best chances of improving the odds for making useful connections is 'tandem reviewing' - which simply involves reviewing both experiences: first the experience from which the action point comes, and secondly the experience to which it might apply.

> After using a suitable reviewing method (such as ANALYTICAL QUESTIONING, CARTOON, HAPPY CHART or WARM SEAT) the similarities and differences between the two experiences are compared. Any action points arising from this process will be built on the common ground that has been discovered through reviewing both experiences.

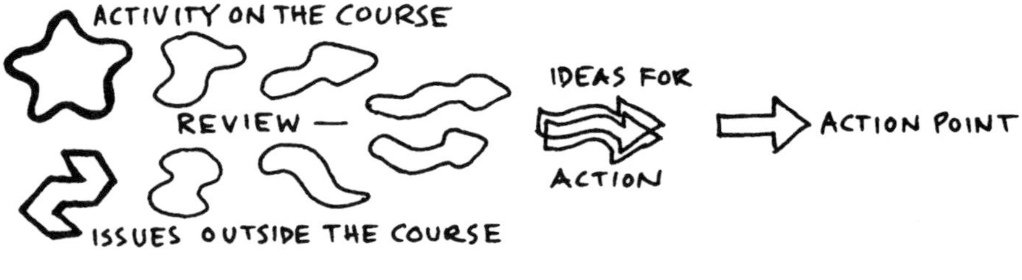

- Commitment to an action point can be increased by rehearsing it through role play.

WARM SEAT

The 'warm seat' generates ideas for action points for the seated person. Unlike the 'hot seat' where individuals are put on the spot and face questions from others, the 'warm seat' is a *comfortable* seat from which the seated person asks the questions. The most important feature of this reviewing method is that *the seated person is in control*: if they feel 'too hot', 'too cold' or in any way uncomfortable, they leave the seat to stop whatever is being said.

> The group will have shared a number of experiences together and they are ready to think about applying what they have learned to situations outside the immediate learning environment.

> The concept of action points is briefly explained, and each person is asked to think of one or two questions to ask the group which will help with ideas for action points. (*How could I be more ...? What should I do if ...? How could I get on better with ...?*)

> Seating is arranged in a horse-shoe facing the 'warm seat'. The first questioner sits in the warm seat and asks a question, which is then clearly written up on a board behind the 'warm seat'. This arrangement focuses the group's attention both on the question and on the questioner.

> If the questioner asks about a situation which is not well known to the group, the reviewer should say: *It will not be easy to answer your question unless you tell us a bit more about ...*

> The questioner may choose to change the question, ask extra questions, or give more information but (assuming there is a time limit for each person's time in the warm seat), the more they talk, the more they reduce the time for answers.

▲ Action points assist the transfer of learning.

▲ An action point demonstrates commitment to a certain course of action. If individuals are clear about what they want to achieve then it is easier for others to provide any support that is needed.

▼ Action points are only one way of transferring learning: some developmental benefits happen without the help of detailed planning.

◆ Individuals or groups can have action points.

Also see: FORCES, LEARNING TO LEARN, OBJECTIVES and QUESTIONS.

ACTION REPLAY involves re-enacting an activity as if a video film of the activity is being replayed. Just as on television, the action is 'played back' either to examine an incident more closely or to replay an event worth celebrating. Action replays can also be used as a fun activity, or as a search technique to find incidents or issues to review more thoroughly. Once the reviewer has demonstrated the possibilities, group members can take it in turns to direct the action. The director has some or all of these 'controls' to play with: REWIND, REPLAY, SELECTED HIGHLIGHTS, FAST FORWARD, PAUSE/FREEZE, CUT TO A DIFFERENT SCENE, CUT AND RE-TAKE A SCENE, PROVIDE COMMENTARY/VOICE OVER, SLOW MOTION, WITH/ WITHOUT SOUND, SOUND EFFECTS, ADVERTISEMENT BREAK, etc.

▲ Familiarity with video and television, means that young people readily understand the language of action replays with little need for further explanation. If action replays capture the imagination of a group, they can become a highly versatile reviewing method.

▼ Directors may find their task difficult - with the result that the 'players' start to rebel or drop out. So encourage directors to experiment but not to be too ambitious at first, and encourage 'players' to co-operate with the director - especially as all will want a co-operative group when it is their turn to be a director.

◆ 'Action replay' is a reviewing method which has many advantages over video work: it is cheaper; it keeps involvement and energy high; it is more convenient and saves time; you can do it almost anywhere; you need no equipment (although some 'props' might be useful); it is an exercise in memory, creativity, and teamwork; and it can provide everyone with a chance of leadership (as director).

VARIATIONS

FANTASY REPLAY: If only it had been like this!
IN THE STYLE OF: Capable groups and directors imitate a particular film or TV style, and replay the same incident from a range of perspectives - each bringing out a different 'side' of the story.
INVESTIGATIVE: Bringing out issues which participants have found difficult to recognise or confront during the activity.
CUTS: If reviewing activities of different subgroups, keep cutting from one scene to another (as in TV soaps).

EXAMPLE: LIVING IN THE CAVE

An action replay can help to create a more complete picture where individuals have had a limited perspective of the whole event:

> *We reviewed the adventure with a 45 minute replay. The walking was replayed on 'fast forward', and 'living in the cave' was 'played through' at the correct speed. In the cave were the lads who went to bed early and sang rugby songs. Outside the cave, around the campfire, were the staff and remaining students. The theme of the replay emerged as being 'sensitivity to others' and the drama centred around the to-ing and fro-ing between the two groups. Some of the 'go-betweens' (staff and students) were trying to create a more homely, sensitive atmosphere in the cave, and other 'go-betweens' were trying to work out which group they belonged to.* [3]

AUDIENCE

If young people are not used to the idea of drama without an audience (and would see more sense if there was one) then try to create an 'audience' when first using the technique. If the group has been working in two subgroups, then an action replay might be a good way for each subgroup to inform the other. If the reviewer has not witnessed the activity to be reviewed, then the group can perform an action replay with the reviewer as the audience. If there seems to be a 'cover up' of some kind that the reviewer wants to 'uncover', improvised action replays tend to reveal what really happened.

ARTS are reviewable activities; they also provide limitless opportunities for reviewing other activities and experiences. Creative methods are particularly suitable for reviewing physical activities such as expeditions or explorations.

These two pages are about the value of the arts in helping young people to express themselves. Other pages provide more detailed examples of reviewing methods which make use of ideas from the creative and performing arts.

USING THE ARTS FOR REVIEWING ACTIVITIES

Using an artistic medium to represent experiences can assist the reviewing of activities in the following ways:

1) the process of creating something *on their own* helps individuals to sort out their own thoughts and feelings, after which they are able to express themselves more clearly;
2) the process of creating something *co-operatively* (in pairs or groups) encourages young people to talk to each other in some depth and detail about their experiences of the activity;
3) whatever is created through art serves as a visual aid or confidence booster in helping young people to communicate their experience of the activity to others;
4) the art form 'speaks for itself', sometimes communicating more about an activity experience than any discussion could achieve.

ART AS A TOOL FOR RAISING AWARENESS

Although art is referred to below as a 'tool', it is seen as one which is an integral part of everyday culture ...

Art is a tool which a variety of Black young people use to communicate with. As our culture is the way we live, and art is a part of that culture, therefore the way we live, the way we move, the way we gesticulate, the way we talk, the way we reason, it's all part of our culture and our art forms. Art, whether it be the pirate station, the sound system, the rap, the dub, the bangra, the acting, the painting or the drawing, or the music, can be used to raise awareness about the particular experiences we go through as Black people. [4]

EXPLORING ISSUES THROUGH ART

An 'artistic medium' can help young people to confront or discuss important issues ...

> *As well as offering opportunities for the cultivation of new skills and interests, the introduction of arts into young people's lives can help them communicate with one another and build up their confidence and self-esteem. The key to successful arts work is recognising that the benefits extend beyond the practical activity - in fact, the activity may simply be a vehicle for introducing a particular theme into youth work. Young people who will not readily confront or discuss issues of importance to them often feel less threatened if such issues are raised through an artistic medium.*

ARTS ACTIVITY AS COLLECTIVE AND INDIVIDUAL SELF-EXPRESSION

> *Higher profile arts activity, whether it is spray can art, poster work, producing a newsletter or making music, inevitably leads to a more positive, more visible presence for youth in the community. The collective and individual self-expression achievable through a whole range of artistic disciplines can present a strong and lasting challenge to the too easily perpetuated negative images of young people which appear in the media and abound in society as a whole.*

YOUNG PEOPLE PRESENTING THEMSELVES AS THEY WOULD WANT TO BE SEEN

> *Posters ... can make succinct and vivid statements about how young people see themselves. Drama and theatre projects involve valuable participative processes as well as community entertainment, and allow young people to express their views in ways that they might not feel comfortable with in everyday life. For groups of young people who identify themselves as oppressed, many art forms give them the opportunity to challenge stereotypes by presenting themselves as they would want to be seen.* [4]

CARDS provide endless possibilities as a reviewing aid. Index cards (slightly larger than playing cards) are ideal for most purposes:
- they are cheap, handy and portable compared with other visual aids;
- they can be written on without needing a hard resting surface;
- they can be readily sorted and arranged in sequences and patterns;
- they can be shuffled, dealt and used in the style of card games.

CHAT CARDS: LISTENING TO, AND REPRESENTING OTHERS

> The group and/or the reviewer generates review questions relating to the previous activity. These are written out, one per card, with the number of cards corresponding to the number of pairs.
> The cards are shuffled and dealt out (one card per pair).
> Pairs discuss the question on the card, for a fixed time (say 2 minutes), then pass the card on.
> Follow up with a group discussion on each question, starting each discussion with the rule: *You may only contribute by representing the views of your partner.*

CARD RACE: AGENDA RAISING AND PRIORITISING

> Everyone has three cards on which to write review questions/topics.
> The cards are spread out face up on the floor.
> Any individual can veto a topic by turning a card face down.
> Cards with similar questions are placed on top of each other.
> The remaining face-up cards (and piles) are lined up for a 'race'.
> Each person moves their 'favourite' question forwards three spaces (e.g. the length of a shoe or the width of a carpet tile), their second favourite two spaces, and their third favourite one space.
> The writer of the winning card initiates discussion on their topic.

SCORE CARDS: MONITORING GROUP ACHIEVEMENTS

Up to ten cards representing 'group goals' are pinned in a row along the foot of a noticeboard. Imagine a vertical column above each card. When a card reaches the top of its column, the goal is achieved. At a suitable point during each review, a group member (a different person each time) is asked to move the cards up or down to show the extent to which that person thinks each 'goal' was achieved. If the scoring is challenged, it is discussed until group consensus is reached.

When this exercise is first introduced, goals might be about keeping to ground rules; achieving programme objectives; or developing group skills such as listening, decision-making and teamwork. New goals can be introduced at any stage: these are likely to be more specific, reflecting recurring issues or relating to new tasks.

JOGGER CARDS: REMINDING INDIVIDUALS OF ACTION POINTS

> From previous reviews, each individual should have at least one personal ACTION POINT relating to their behaviour during activities, such as: 'I should speak up more', 'listen more', 'not give up easily'.

> Up to three action points per person are recorded on 'jogger' cards (as in 'memory jogger') and given to an 'observer' for the next activity. The more cards there are, the more observers will be needed.

> During the next activity, observers look out for individuals who do not appear to be implementing their action points, and unobtrusively show them the appropriate card.

> Any disputes about this feedback are postponed until after the activity.

CREDIT CARDS: AN APPRAISAL GAME

Each card has a short phrase such as: *you tried hardest; you surprised me most; you laughed the most; you were the most predictable; you helped me most; you cared most about others;* etc.

Also known as 'COMPUTER CARDS', this popular appraisal game, in which people pass each other cards with ready-made messages on them, is very *un*popular with individuals who receive a pile of negative cards. (There are better and more sensitive ways of providing critical feedback). Even if played with cards with only positive messages, those who receive no cards at all do not feel very positive! This game works best when the reviewer knows the group very well and can confidently predict (a) who will get which cards and (b) how individuals will respond to what they are likely to receive. This game works well as a reviewing technique if the cards refer to specific events during the activity being reviewed. [5]

As a reviewing method, drawing a strip CARTOON helps young people to tell the 'story' of what happened during an activity stage by stage. Creating the cartoon can also be used as a means of planning the scenes and the basic script for an ACTION REPLAY.

DRAWING AN 'OUTSIDE' PROBLEM

▲ Cartoons are a useful means for individuals to inform other group members about difficulties, dilemmas, challenges or other kinds of problem which they have experienced outside the group. Once other members of the group can 'picture' what happened, and can 'see' the sequence of events, they will find it easier to help the individual to review the experience.

> Young people could be interested in problems which are 'unique' to just one group member, but it is more productive to concentrate on problems which are similar to those others have experienced (or might experience). Depending on the membership and purposes of the group, situations suitable for cartooning might be incidents relating to:

problems at school, training, work; an interview; unemployment; being assertive; setting up a new home; being bullied; getting into trouble; playing a sport; working with elderly people; organising a youth club; fundraising; campaigning; etc.

> As the cartoon will be shown to the group, encourage large drawings (even if matchstick figures). By using an A4 sized sheet for each frame, there is the added advantage that mistakes on individual frames do not spoil the whole strip - they are readily discarded and redrawn.

> As the purpose is to trace the events leading up to the problem in the final frame, 'cartoonists' are advised to start with the last frame and work backwards.

> The normal convention in strip cartoons is to introduce separate strands of the story with 'Meanwhile...'; a useful alternative for reviewing purposes is to arrange them so that they converge into a single strip (like railway sidings converging into one main line).

EXAMINING AN 'OUTSIDE' PROBLEM

> Group members may first need to ask questions about the cartoon for clarification. Such questions also help the 'cartoonist' understand more about the situation they are presenting.

> This is the point where an ACTION REPLAY directed by the 'cartoonist' can be an effective means of telling the story. Participants

in the replay will first need their parts explained. The 'cartoonist' (now the 'director') either plays their own part in the replay, or asks someone else to do so. The 'director' can gain a new perspective of the situation by playing the part of another person in the story. (Ensure everyone has 'switched off' from the part they were playing before continuing.)

> Once everyone has a reasonably clear picture of what happened, the young person sharing the problem asks a question such as:

- *What could/should I have done differently?*
- *What could/should I do to prevent this happening again?*
- *If I get into this situation again what could/should I do?*

> During the ensuing discussion, it is useful to refer to, alter, re-draw or re-arrange the cartoon frames.

> If action replay was used, drama is now easily reintroduced to look forward - to 'test' or 'rehearse' any alternatives suggested. [6]

MORE USES FOR CARTOONS

ACTION POINTS: Using strip cartoons to describe situations outside the group to which ACTION POINTS might apply.

DIFFERENT PERSPECTIVES: Ask each individual to produce (privately) a strip cartoon of the same group event, then discuss variations.

RE-UNITING: If a group has not met for a while, or if young people have been on their own, or in subgroups, then their various stories can be told through cartoons.

CARTOON TAPESTRY: Cartoon strips are regularly produced throughout a course and as each one is completed they are joined end to end in a 'tapestry' - telling the story of the group as it unfolds.

GROUP DISCUSSION is the most fundamental reviewing technique of all. Most of the methods described in this chapter involve group discussion and will add to the quality of such reviews. These two pages provide some ideas for reviewing group discussions, and some 'gimmicks' for encouraging more equal participation.

REVIEWING GROUP DISCUSSIONS

As discussion is likely to be the most frequently used reviewing method, it is well worth spending time reviewing it!

> Ask group members to make three separate lists of what they have found PLUS, MINUS AND INTERESTING about the review discussions so far.

> Ask: "How can our discussions be improved?" ... "Which of these ideas shall we try out for our next review discussion?"

> Also ask each person to come up with two action points which will help them to GIVE AND GET more in future discussions. If individuals are stuck for ideas, ask others to make suggestions.

> If the idea is being promoted that reviewer and participants share responsibility for the quality of discussions, then it is logical for the reviewer to end up with their own action points.

> Revising GROUND RULES [page 21] may also be a useful exercise.

EQUAL OPPORTUNITIES TO PARTICIPATE

It will be surprising if this is not (in some form) high on the agenda for improving the quality of review discussions in a group. Several methods for tackling this problem are described here, but ...

▼ ... all the methods are intrusive and in most circumstances are probably best used as a *temporary but memorable gimmick*, rather than as 'normal' procedure for discussions.

PARTICIPATION LINE-UP: Ask the group to LINE UP with the person who participates most at one end, the person who participates least at the other, with everyone else in order in between. Group members now sit in order in a 'C'. When using ROUNDS, the 'quietest' person has the first chance to participate, and the 'loudest' completes the round.

MATCHSTICKS: Ask the group to try this for the first part of the review. Each person has (say) 5 safety matches. Throwing a match into a bucket in the middle stops the speaker immediately and allows the interrupter to speak until another match is thrown in. When somebody runs out of matches, decide very quickly whether (a) to stick rigidly to the rules; (b) to be flexible and allow the group to revise the rules; (c) to abandon 'matchsticks' altogether.

THE CONCH: During the island meetings in William Golding's 'Lord of the Flies', only the holder of the conch shell is allowed to speak. The 'conch' (any item, but 'precious' rather than 'throwable') can be used to control group discussion. To ensure equal opportunities for participation, the rule is that the conch is always passed to the left, and is quickly passed on if the holder has nothing to say. Every few minutes (or after every round), there is a random swapping of seats, so that the sequence of speakers is changed.

BALL OF WOOL: A ball of wool which unwinds as it is passed from speaker to speaker can reveal interesting patterns, (but can also become so intrusive that everyone drifts off the original subject and ends up talking about wool). An alternative is for an observer to draw (unobtrusively) the course that the wool would have followed.

QUESTION AND ANSWER ONLY: The only contributions allowed are questions or answers.

SUMMARISE FIRST: Anyone who wishes to speak must first summarise (or at least refer to) what the previous speaker said.

GOLDFISH BOWL: Half the group sits in an inner circle and review the activity while the other half sits in the outer circle and listen. When the reviewer calls 'swap', seats are changed and the new inner circle continues with the review after providing a quick summary of the main points made by the previous inner circle.

MIXING THE GROUP: Experiment with different sized groups [page 21].

EVALUATION can be applied to all stages of a learning cycle and to all aspects of a programme, including inputs, processes and outcomes. Evaluation can be a short term process affecting immediate decisions about how to proceed, or it can be a longer term process, the findings of which (if applied) will influence other events with other young people. The evaluation methods described on these pages can be used at any stage of a course or programme.

SOME PRINCIPLES

> Keep a dialogue going with young people about the course.
> Be clear about what you are evaluating and why.
> Make time for doing so, and get the support you need.
> Discuss your plans and findings with others to get a wider view.
> For end of course evaluation, find a suitable balance between:
- a standardised approach to evaluation (which allows comparisons);
- a tailor-made approach (specific to a particular programme);
- and an open-ended, creative approach (which may pick up important insights that more systematic approaches overlook).

SOME 'CREATIVE' EXAMPLES

PLUS, MINUS, INTERESTING (PMI) is one of Edward de Bono's methods for evaluating ideas. Introducing a lateral ("interesting") dimension makes evaluation a more creative and constructive process. 'PMI' is a useful way of providing feedback about ideas, experiences or people.

PICTURES: Draw/paint pictures or diagrams representing what you have learned and how you have benefitted. The pictures can be abstract or realistic; they can show yourself, others, activities, fantasy...

BALANCES: What have you found to be *TOO MUCH? ... NOT ENOUGH? ... JUST RIGHT ...?* After each answer, give reasons why.

COURSE DESIGN: For 'creative' feedback: ask the group to redesign the course (so far) for a similar group on a similar occasion; or ask them to design an extension of the course for a few more sessions.

EVALUATING ACTIVITIES: BEYOND ENJOYMENT!

It is difficult to evaluate activities if there are no clear criteria against which to evaluate them other than 'enjoyment' - which is where this method starts.

> Make a list of all the activities in which young people have taken part, roughly in the order of the total time spent doing each one.

> Hand out copies, and ask individuals to show how much they *enjoyed* each activity by giving a mark out of ten *in front of each* word.

> Write the first activity on a flipchart and ask what people did or did not enjoy about it. Record these 'factors affecting enjoyment' beside each activity. Repeat this process, working down the list of activities until there are no new factors being suggested.

> Now ask the group to choose the ten most relevant factors - that is the ten which are most closely linked to the aims of the programme. (If the aims are not clear, then ask which ten factors they think have most affected their learning and development.)

> Individuals now refer to their own copies of the list and, after each activity listed, they give a mark out of ten to show *how many* of the ten factors applied to their experience of the activity in question.

> Scores can now be interpreted in subgroups or in the whole group. For example, do any activities have a high enjoyment score but a low relevance score (or vice versa)?

▲ This step by step method helps to make young people's own criteria more explicit. These factors can then be applied in a systematic way to the activities which they have experienced.

▼ If young people are not in the habit of reviewing, they may find it difficult to analyse what they enjoyed about an activity.

◆ This method produces interesting statistics, but the session as a whole, especially the discussion arising from the statistics, should also be taken into account when evaluating activities or a course.

◆ Some reviewing activities could themselves be evaluated, but the main evidence of the value of reviewing will be in the degree to which young people can make evaluative judgements in areas other than enjoyment.

'FORCES' is used here as an umbrella term to refer to reviewing methods which are loosely based on 'force field analysis'.

The basic concept of 'force field analysis' is that, where forces are in opposition, there are two basic strategies for bringing about positive change: (1) increasing positive forces and (2) decreasing negative forces. The first stage of any such analysis involves identifying and mapping the forces involved.

GROUP SNAKES AND LADDERS

> After an activity involving teamwork, make two lists with the group. One list (the LADDERS) is of all the factors (tiny or enormous) that in some way helped the group to work better as a team. The second list (the SNAKES) is of all the factors that in some way hindered teamwork. (Factors can include words, actions, feelings etc.)
> Try to extend the LADDERS list by checking whether the forces opposing each snake are listed. Then try to extend the SNAKES list by checking whether the forces threatening each ladder are listed.
> Now cut up the lists (or transfer them onto cards) and ask half the group to rank-order the snakes, and the other half to rank-order the ladders - placing the force which was *most influential* during the activity at the top of each rank-order.
> The snakes and ladders are now lined up in single rows (in order) opposite each other, and the group are asked to discuss, "How can our teamwork improve?" (If some forces are expressed in a way that is too specific to the previous activity, then try generalising them into a force that could be relevant to future activities.)
> If the discussion needs focusing, ask for two group ACTION POINTS to build on positive forces and two group action points to reduce negative forces. Individual action points may also be relevant.
> If the activity merits an extended review, then making a giant 'artistic' version of the board game can be an interesting end product. Playing the game is a possibility, but could be overkill!

INDIVIDUAL SNAKES AND LADDERS

More individual themes can be analysed using a similar process - themes such as 'enjoyment', 'confidence' or 'MOTIVATION' ...

> First list any forces (internal or external) that affected anyone's motivation during the activity being reviewed. Point out that the same forces may be a snake for one person, but a ladder for another.

> Individuals select and rank-order their own snakes and their own ladders, and then try to find the people in the room who have the most different and the most similar patterns of forces.

> Whether there is a reasonably wide spread of patterns represented in the group, or whether everyone has much the same pattern, discuss what the implications are for ensuring that everyone is more motivated in future activities.

INDIVIDUAL FORCE FIELDS

This method applies to regularly experienced events, whether these are activities or any other aspects of a young person's life. When working with individuals who face recurring difficulties in their lives, and who are stuck in a rut, it can be particularly useful to map out the 'force-field' surrounding them. To minimise the chances of this being a thoroughly depressing exercise which cements the individual more firmly in place, it is important for the young person to have first experienced the successful use of a 'force-field' review in a group setting. Not only will the young person then know how it works, they will also have had first hand evidence that it does work.

> Once the mapping of forces has been carried out, ask the young person to rank-order each set of forces, giving 10 points maximum to the most influential force, down to 1 for the least influential force.

> Ask the young person to estimate how difficult it will be to change any of these forces in the desired direction (from 1 = 'I have no power to improve this' to 10 = 'I have the power to improve this').

> Multiply the two scores for each force. This crude calculation should help individuals to decide which forces to work on, and should discourage them from wasting their efforts on low-scoring choices which are either too challenging or too marginal.

> Group support, if available, can greatly assist this process.

GIFTS

'GIFTS' is an appraisal activity in which young people make, find or mime gifts for each other. The qualities represented by the gifts should have been in evidence during the activity being reviewed. The session should be arranged so that 'appreciative' gifts outweigh 'critical' gifts: each example provided below has two positive messages and one negative message.

These are some of the options for setting up a 'gift' session:

OPTION 1) Divide the group in two, and ask each subgroup to prepare gifts for individuals in the other subgroup.

OPTION 2) Interview group members one at a time (perhaps for one-to-one reviewing) while the rest of the group is preparing a gift for that person.

OPTION 3) Ask individuals or pairs to prepare gifts for everyone else in the group, with the result that each individual receives several gifts.

MAKING GIFTS

An example of a 'made' gift: light blue paper (representing calm) on which is drawn an outline of someone's hands (representing help), above which is a photograph of a bird cut out from a magazine. The giver of the gift explains what it means:

"We admired you for your courage when trying to rescue the bird, but we wish you wouldn't go it alone so much, and had asked us to help. (This is *your* hand helping the bird. This is *our* helping hand which you didn't ask for in time.) We admired you for staying calm (the blue) when you needed rescuing."

Making three dimensional gifts (e.g. robots, pets, toys, hats, brains) gives greater scope, but is more time-consuming.

FINDING GIFTS

Define an area within which gifts can be found (inside, outside or both) and ask pairs to find one gift for each other person in the group. Explain that the gift should represent two positive messages and one critical message. Here are two examples:

1) "Here is some *sticky tape* to help you keep your mouth shut, such as when .... We hope you will find it useful for other things because you are clearly a very practical

person in the way you ... And it represents your humour which helped us to *stick* together as a group."

2) "This *fir cone* is you because you would just lie around doing nothing if we didn't make you join in. All the bits sticking out show the talents you've got but don't use enough - like problem-solving, singing, mimicking other people. And there are bugs crawling around inside because you're friendly to everyone: people always come to you if they need someone to talk to."

MIMING GIFTS

If you can't find the right object you can always mime it! Also, mime allows absolutely any object to be a gift (however big or expensive):

"Here is a *motorbike* (wheelie mime) because you show off a lot - like when you said you could do canoeing, but you were the first to fall in. Here is a private *jet* (flying mime) for going on holidays whenever you want to, because when you're doing activities and things, it makes you happy and a much nicer person to know. Here is a *lumberjack's axe* (chopping mime) because you work really hard and put a lot of effort in - not just the exciting things, but chores as well."

BALANCED APPRAISAL

In all of the examples above, each giver gives one negative message and two positive ones, which seems to be the right kind of balance in most appraisal work. Such a balance arguably has a more constructive impact than using a 'positive only' rule - which results in positive comments seeming forced and insincere. Such a balance also means that people are likely to be less defensive when receiving criticism. Perhaps this 2:1 positive balance will result in receivers' self-esteem taking two steps forward and one step back. You can check the impact by asking young people afterwards whether they feel 'knocked back' or 'lifted'. The chances are that young people are used to getting knocked back by peer group 'humour', and that it is the rare experience of *positive* appraisal that has had the greatest impact.

In GUIDED REFLECTION, participants listen while the reviewer talks through what happened in a way which prompts reflection.

It is a useful introduction to a reviewing session and is an efficient use of reviewing time. In only a few minutes everyone can 're-live' experiences in their minds. With suitable prompts from the reviewer, they can 're-view' their experiences from new angles.

SETTING UP

To avoid distractions, participants should be in a comfortable position and have their eyes closed. For a quick version of this method (say 2-3 minutes) group members sitting in a circle simply turn round and face outwards. For deeper, more sustained reflection (say 10-15 minutes) it is better for participants to lie down and relax.

INTRODUCTION

The reviewer explains the method. For example:

A lot of things have happened since the activity began. This is a chance for you to sort out your thoughts and feelings, by re-living the activity in your mind. I will talk through the activity, asking questions and pausing. The questions are for answering inside your head. The idea of this exercise is that you will have a few minutes collecting your own thoughts before we review the activity in a more sociable way. Let's start ...

TELLING THE STORY

The reviewer talks through what happened, describing events and asking questions. The present tense brings it alive. For example:

We are in the minibus on the way to the dropping off point ... It's raining ... Laura says she feels sick ... David says he's seen a golden eagle and no-one believes him ... Now it's quiet for a while ... Do you remember what you were thinking at the time? Were you thinking about the eagle, or about what lay ahead, or about something else?

SAMPLE QUESTIONS

The questions asked during the 'story' may highlight one or two themes that the reviewer wants to emphasise, and can apply to any stage of the reviewing sequence (Chapter 1). For example:

- MOTIVATION AND ORIENTATION: *Did you make up your mind beforehand about how you would approach the activity? What was most on your mind when it started? Did you have any personal targets or responsibilities to carry out during the activity?*
- PREDICTIONS AND SURPRISES: *Did you predict what would happen in any way? Did you think about what part you or others would play? Did things turn out as you expected? Was there anything that surprised you about the activity ... about yourself ... about others?*
- REGRETS AND ACHIEVEMENTS: *Think about the things you did that affected others - things you were pleased you did and things you wish you hadn't done. Think of what you didn't do but meant to. Think about what you were trying to achieve, and what you did achieve.*
- APPRECIATION: *Have you helped others in any way and not been thanked or appreciated? Do you owe thanks to others? Who to? Why?*
- NEXT TIME: *How could/would you or the group do things differently next time - to make it better for you and for everyone else?*

▲ If it was a long activity, or some time has elapsed since, then guided reflection can help to remind people of key events and of issues they may want to raise later.

▲ Issues may also arise if the reviewer includes some thought-provoking questions (and remembers to ask for responses later on).

▲ Well-timed pauses following well-phrased questions allow young people to think honestly and deeply about their experiences.

▲ If the reviewer follows a 'script' that applies to everyone, any number of people can take part in this method.

▼ Guided reflection is one-way communication, so it is difficult for the reviewer to know whether they are going too fast or too slow, or whether the technique is working at all ... so it is advisable for the reviewer to find out soon afterwards what impact the method has had.

◆ Practice with known groups will help the reviewer to judge the pace, and to find the right level and frequency of questions.

HUMAN SCULPTURE is an active way of looking at patterns and relationships in a group. The method can be used to highlight differences within a group at various times during the activity.

All the 'sculptures' described here start with 'POSITIONING'. To do this, imagine that the floor space is a giant target with a bulls-eye at the centre. The low-scoring perimeter of the target can be marked out by a boundary rope, or by a circle of chairs. Individuals position themselves in relation to whatever the centre is chosen to represent. This provides the basic pattern which can then be adjusted and developed in various ways to create a 'human sculpture'.

▲ Human sculptures are a simple, visual concept which instantly involve everyone. No materials are needed. The technique can be used indoors or outdoors. The first stage (positioning) provides a quick snapshot of how individuals saw themselves during the activity. The second stage (sculpting) allows participants to move each other's position (and posture) as a means of providing feedback on how they saw each other during the activity.

▼ A sculpture can be misinterpreted or can exaggerate what really happened, so it is important to encourage people to speak up, especially if there are signs of disagreement or discomfort. Equally, it should be emphasised that the purpose is not to fix things in stone but to find out what people want to *change* or *improve*: they are not stone sculptures; they are *human* sculptures. This message can be emphasised by sculpting a likely future event in a way which demonstrates changes that people want to make.

◆ Sometimes, the principal value of sculptures comes from the strong visual images that are created; at other times it comes from the conversations that are sparked off by the positions and postures.

Be prepared for either.

VARIATIONS

Three basic variations are described below. The first is the most straightforward and therefore a good way to introduce sculptures. The 'individual' and 'symbolic' approaches require more intitiative and imagination from participants.

THEMES: The centre of the circle can represent any theme related to personal or group development: *enthusiasm, effort, humour, involvement, listening to others, influence, leadership, co-operation, giving and receiving support, giving and receiving criticism, initiative, responsibility, risk-taking, value to the group, etc.* Sometimes it is useful to race through several subjects. At other times, it pays to explore one subject in detail. For example, people with low self-esteem tend to place themselves towards the edge of the circle for 'value to the group': this should prompt others to invite them closer in to the centre, giving a reason for doing so.

INDIVIDUAL: The centre can also represent a member of the group. If individuals are to set up their own sculptures (about how they saw others relating to them during the activity), some individual preparation time (to sketch people's positions) saves time during the 'sculpting' stage. Imaginative use of sculpture should be encouraged. For example, an individual might want to say to another:

> *You kept telling me what to do, but you never seemed to notice the problems I was having, so stand close to me but face outwards, and keep calling out, 'Sheila, do this. Sheila do that.'*

SYMBOLIC: A symbolic sculpture can be a good way for an individual to present a personal dilemma that was experienced during the activity. The pressures, conflicts and possible courses of action, from the *sculptor's* perspective, can be represented by the 'sculptor' positioning others around them (in suitable poses). "These were the kind of things going on *inside my mind* when I was trying to decide what to do." This is also a particularly good method for introducing a dilemma experienced outside the group - during work placement, on the street, at school, at home, doing Award activities, etc.

Good quality reviewing does not always depend on the presence of a reviewer: there are many situations in which INDEPENDENT REVIEWING is a useful alternative, including:
- where a group is becoming too dependent on the reviewer;
- where there is so much going on in a group that individuals need to take time to reflect on their own, or to review in smaller groups;
- in order to complete journals, diaries, reports, or questionnaires;
- where there is no time to review after an activity, so participants are asked to complete a reviewing task before they next meet;
- where young people are being encouraged to take more responsibility for reviewing (as part of their training for committee work, or in preparation for an independent expedition);
- where 'empowerment' or 'developing learning skills' are objectives;
- where there is a need to review in subgroups but there are not enough staff to go round;
- when the reviewer needs a break, or has run out of ideas!

In the review tasks described below, the end product is described, but how it is produced is mostly left to the group's discretion. The group are asked either to produce something within a specified time, or to keep working until the task is completed.

ACTION POINTS: List the five most surprising things that happened during the last activity; list five aspects of teamwork which were particularly good; and list five ACTION POINTS for the group which will help you to improve the quality of your teamwork.

ACTION REPLAYS: Practise two ACTION REPLAYS, one which highlights what went well, and one which highlights what didn't go well. Incorporate these into a five minute performance on the theme of 'Past and Future' which ends with a 'preview' of the next activity.

ART: Make a collage/sculpture/junk model about the last activity, showing a mixture of 'obvious' and 'not-so-obvious' experiences associated with the activity.

GROUP POEM: Using six blank cards, each individual writes down three words and three phrases about the previous activity. As a group, arrange all of these words and phrases together to produce a group poem about the activity (using a few extra words if needed).

GROUP SONG: Write and perform a song about the last activity which mentions and involves everyone in the group.

NEWS REPORT: produce a front page newspaper story, a RADIO NEWS item (on tape), or a VIDEO about the last activity.

PREPARATION FOR APPRAISAL: described in REPORTS and GIFTS.

QUESTIONNAIRES: A QUESTIONNAIRE relating to the previous activity is handed out to each person, and is completed individually. The notes made during this individual review exercise are then used for a review discussion. The reviewer should announce at the start if individuals will be asked to read out any of their answers.

REVIEW DISCUSSION (PREPARATION): (for a group of ten) The group agree a five part agenda for reviewing the activity, and then divide into five pairs, with each pair choosing to lead one item on the agenda. Each pair then has (say) five minutes preparation time.

REVIEW DISCUSSION (OBSERVED BY REVIEWER): The group prepares for a review discussion which will take place in the presence of a non-participating reviewer. (Alternatively the reviewer helps a 'trainee' reviewer to prepare for chairing the discussion.) The reviewer describes their own role clearly - which may be "to observe and record, but unlikely to intervene". At a suitable point, such as 'half-time' or at the end, the reviewer provides feedback on the review process, in the group setting or one-to-one.

This LABELLING exercise enables young people to experience what it is like to be in other people's shoes.

> *Young people's development is held back if people around them are not letting them change or grow up: they may have liked them too much as they used to be, or they may have written them off, perhaps labelling them as 'trouble-maker', 'slow learner' or 'failure'. Young people may be unlucky enough to live in a world ... in which whatever they do gets explained by themselves or by others in terms of outdated stories or labels from the past.* [7]

In this exercise, the term 'labelling' is used both in its metaphorical sense of stereotyping and in its literal sense: participants wear real labels. Participants do not attempt to act out the role on their labels: they experience the roles as a result of the ways in which others react to the labels they are wearing.

REVIEW OF THE PREVIOUS ACTIVITY AND MAKING LABELS FOR THE NEXT ONE

> Assisted by the group, draw up a list of roles (good, bad or in between) which were evident during the previous activity/activities.
> Each individual then chooses from the list a role which they are not accustomed to, and which they are interested in experiencing.
> Using a large sticky label, this role is displayed clearly on the forehead. (Or use large luggage labels tied in a prominent place.)

DURING THE NEXT ACTIVITY: REACTING TO LABELS

> Everyone tries to behave as themselves and tries to avoid conforming to the role on their label. The only 'acting' involved is in reacting (but not over-reacting) to others according to what is written on other people's labels.
> It is important to emphasise to participants that individuals can opt out at any time they want (if, for example they get fed up with being treated as a 'scapegoat' or a 'moaner'). Also warn that the reviewer may stop the exercise at any time, or change someone's label (by sticking a new one on top or changing the tie-on luggage label).

REVIEWING LABELS AND LABELLING

> The review starts with each person saying what it was like being treated 'As if I was a ...' (i.e. whatever was on their label). Some will have very pleasant experiences to report, others may not have enjoyed the experience. Both kinds of experiences should be followed up in discussion, the purpose of which is to consider the effects of 'labelling' people.

> Ideally the group will choose to adopt ACTION POINTS which discourage the 'labelling' of others and which support experimentation with new roles and responsibilities. If after this discussion anyone is still 'down' from the experience, it may help to underline what has been learned, and then to see whether any apologies are due.

> Ask everyone to choose a pleasant label for the next activity - to harness the power of 'positive' labelling (although 'positive' reactions to 'pleasant' labels are not guaranteed).

▲ An advantage of this labelling exercise is that it is suitable for groups new to drama-based techniques. Unlike 'role reversal' exercises, it only requires *some* acting ability by some members of the group in order to create an experience of what a different role can be like, but ...

▼ ... inexperienced actors may find it difficult to switch out of a role once they have got into it - so help them to switch off!

ACTING + ACTIVITY = ?

The combination of 'acting' and 'activity' can be an unpredictable one. The activity the labelling exercise is linked to should be an engrossing but fairly easy activity with a wide safety margin. Also, the activity should be in a safe area so that it can be monitored readily. The reviewer should try to ensure that there are sufficient positive labels for the activity to be completed successfully in the end. If necessary, the balance can be adjusted by changing the labels during the activity. Ideally, the choice of activity would result in participants' attention being more or less equally divided between the 'activity' and the 'acting'.

For many young people, the most lasting impact of activity-based learning is that they are LEARNING TO LEARN in new ways.

There are many features of reviewing (even in its most basic form) which are fundamentally different from the typical messages about learning that are picked up in school, or from educational television. Instead of there being a body of knowledge 'out there' being poured into young inexperienced people, it suddenly happens (in activity-based learning) that young people's own experiences become the centre of attention.

The belief underlying this approach is that people learn best from what they themselves experience. In order to learn from what they experience, people first need to have suitable kinds of experiences - in the area in which they want to learn or develop. These experiences then need to be suitably reviewed in order to initiate or accelerate the process of learning from the experience.

It is likely that young people's first sustained exposure to activity-based learning will be such a new experience that it will be difficult for them to step outside it and understand the process. But every effort should be made to ensure that young people do not just take part in activities but also take an active and responsible part in the learning process. The two methods described below can help young people understand more about the learning process, and so discover how to become more active learners.

A MODEL OF LEARNING:

The reviewer needs to find a way of presenting the learning process outlined above (or a version of it) - not just what it is, or how it works, but also WHY this particular process is so vitally important. A simple two-stage learning cycle showing 'DOING' and 'REVIEWING' is a useful visual aid (See p 11). It is also helpful to involve the group in an active demonstration of the process using a short activity and a short, 'fail-safe' reviewing method - such as ROUNDS.

REVIEWING TO DEVELOP LEARNING SKILLS

This example is based on ski training, but can be readily used with any session involving the teaching of activity skills. Where young people really want to *learn* to ski, then it makes sense to give some attention to *learning* methods as well as to skiing methods.

> Before setting off to the slope give each learner a record which lists different ways of learning. The list might include the following:

watching a good demonstration; receiving encouragement; being told what I'm doing wrong; playing games; experimenting (without instruction); being taught by another learner; teaching another learner; repeated practice of one exercise; trying a new skill; practising in more difficult conditions; practising in easier conditions; journeying (keeping on the move) ...

> After the session give these written instructions to group members:
- Tick the learning methods in the list which you yourself experienced during the session, and add any that are missing.
- Score each learning method you experienced on a scale 0 - 10 to show how helpful you found each method during that particular session. Explain and discuss your scoring with a partner.

> At the next group review, look at the variations between how different people like to learn to ski. How much is this variation (in preferred ways of learning) to do with confidence, skiing ability, motivation, etc.?

> Discuss how individuals like to learn other new skills. How is learning to ski similar and different from learning these other skills?

> If individuals keep all their records, it is then useful to review how their experiences and preferences changed over the whole period of their skiing lessons.

◆ This approach to reviewing was first devised in order to make better use of the minibus journey back from regular skiing sessions. The paired conversations can be carried out during the journey.

◆ The more the instructor is involved in (or at least informed about) this reviewing process, the more likely it is that the instructor will end up with the best learners and the winning skiing class!

METAPHORS extend the power of words and phrases by using them out of their original context. Metaphor is deeply rooted in our language; our ancestors used to describe each other in terms of the animals which they resembled. This ancient custom has been resurrected in the form of an appraisal game called 'animal metaphors'! The examples below show more ways in which metaphorical thinking can be encouraged in reviewing activities. The habit of metaphorical thinking improves young people's ability to make connections and to transfer what they learn from one situation to another.

METAPHOR PORTRAITS

> Introduce the idea with WEATHER metaphors. Ask the group to list different kinds of weather. Then ask which kinds of weather people use to talk about each other (*warm? cold? frosty? ray of sunshine? lightning? stormy? brilliant?*). Then ask if there are any kinds of weather listed which could *NOT* be used to describe someone (extremely unlikely!).

> Ask the group to think of each person's behaviour during the last activity, and to suggest a kind of weather to match (e.g. "I thought you were a *dark cloud* to start with, but a *whirlwind* when time was running out".) After listening to suggestions, individuals can respond by suggesting another kind of weather they think more closely resembled their behaviour during the activity.

> Now divide the group in two, and ask each subgroup to prepare a METAPHOR PORTRAIT for each person in the other sub-group, using at least five types of metaphor (e.g. *animal, colour, electrical appliance, fabric, food, fruit, machine, plant, vehicle, weather*). The metaphors can be written or illustrated, or both. A COLOUR metaphor is a good starting point - especially if coloured paper is available.

> When the whole group re-assembles, each subgroup takes it in turns to present one 'metaphor portrait' at a time. Recipients should be encouraged (but not forced) to respond, perhaps by saying what they find 'fair', 'unfair', 'confusing', 'surprising' etc.

TEAMWORK METAPHORS

Where an activity has involved teamwork, it is possible to make use of teamwork language and concepts that are already familiar to young people. The example given here is based on football.

> *"If this group had been a football team, who would have been captain? Who would have been striker, sweeper, mid-field, goalkeeper? Was anyone referee, coach or spectator? Was anyone sent off?"*

A group that is keen on football can sort out their 'positions' surprisingly quickly, and will often come up with new ideas for 'positions' or 'playing styles' that suit each other.

> Encourage explanations of the suggestions made. Invite individuals to suggest alternative 'positions' for themselves.

> Once a person's position is agreed, they go to it (on or around a small, imaginary football field).

> *"Now we've got the individual 'positions' sorted out, look at the team as a whole. What kind of football team would this be? ... Do the things you have said also apply to the activity we are reviewing?"*

EXTENDABLE METAPHORS

The football team example above is an example of an extendable metaphor within which there are further possibilities for making metaphorical connections. To find other suitable metaphors to extend, listen out for any connections that young people make between the activity and something else (like a TV programme). Also listen out for metaphors in young people's conversation - they may be particularly good ones to work with! For example, the statement "I felt out of my depth" could be part of a swimming pool metaphor ...

> Ask the group to imagine that the room (or review space) is a swimming pool. Show them where the edges, shallow end, and deep end are, and ask them to get 'in the right place' for particular stages of the experience under review.

> Encourage the group to use the metaphor creatively, and not simply to see this as a spectrum from shallow involvement to deep involvement. Perhaps the experience felt like 'fighting for breath', 'learning a new stroke', 'shivering', 'splashing' or 'floating'.

Also see 'Visual Metaphors' in *Creative Drama* by Sue Jennings. [8]

At an early stage, when the reviewer is trying to establish the value of reviewing, it can be useful to interrupt an activity with a review.

Groups often do not fully appreciate why they are reviewing, however much the purpose has been discussed or however much the group has set their own reviewing objectives (although both these strategies help). Interrupting an activity need not be obtrusive, as it can coincide with a natural break or resting point. A mid-activity review has a clearly understood purpose, because some of the learning can be immediately applied. Although it is important to establish connections across activities (as well as within activities), mid-activity reviewing can be an important step towards this goal.

HALF-TIME

Bring out (and give) positive comments for good teamwork and for individuals who have done well in the 'first half'. Consider revising strategy, tactics, positions or roles for the 'second half'.

COMMENTARY

During an activity, individuals can make a running commentary on their experiences to a partner.

PAIRS

At a break in the activity, learners can talk in pairs about the part they've played so far, and share (and record) PREDICTIONS about what they will do next and what will happen.

QUESTIONNAIRES

Mid-activity questionnaires produce notes that can be used for an end-of-activity review. They can also help to focus attention on specific issues during the second part of the activity.

OBSERVERS

In preparation for a later review, 'OBSERVERS' can take it in turns to withdraw from the activity and make notes, or do tape- or video-recording.

Interrupting discussion with action can help to keep a group alert. More interestingly, an 'active' interruption can help a group clarify, test out or visualise something that has been said...

CHECKING THE FACTS

If there are differences of opinion about what actually happened, or if critical events were not witnessed by everyone in the group, then an ACTION REPLAY can help to clarify what happened, or identify the issue more clearly.

CHANGING THE PAST

"So you would like this group to be more trusting? Let's see what that might be like. Let's 'replay' the part(s) of the activity where you weren't very trusting and try to be more trusting this time round."

However this replay works out, it should provide a fresh perspective on the issue, and a more detailed picture of what is possible.

TESTING ASSERTIONS

Some assertions made during a review can be tested out immediately. If someone says, "We are very trusting in this group" or, "We are not very trusting in this group", this could be a good cue for a trust exercise to test this out. It may be a fairly crude test, but it will at least highlight the issue and provide a fresh angle from which to consider it. Similarly, an assertion that "We do listen to each other" or "We are not very good at listening to each other", can be a cue for a listening exercise. It is useful to anticipate likely review issues and have a few quick exercises 'ready for action'.

VISUALISING AN ACTION POINT

It is sometimes useful to act out proposals about future action. This might be because the reviewer can see a problem, but would prefer group members to discover it for themselves. A rehearsal will, in any case, help to check and adjust an ACTION POINT, and increase commitment to it.

Whether the purpose of the activity is broad or specific, the review will need to have at least one clear OBJECTIVE.

If a review does not have a clear objective at the start, then an early priority is to establish one. If a purpose cannot be found, there is clearly no point in proceeding with a review. In such situations, the priority is to track down the reason why objectives are difficult to find and to do something about it.

This subject is also considered in Chapter 2 (PURPOSES) and in the section on objectives in Chapter 5 (ISSUES).

▲ Setting an objective, achieving it and receiving praise and recognition for doing so is an empowering experience!

▲ Objectives help to provide continuity and development throughout what might otherwise be a random assortment of activities.

▲ Objectives enable connections to be made between activity-based learning and issues or opportunities outside the programme.

▼ Reviews dominated by objectives tend to short-circuit the four-stage reviewing sequence (described in Chapter 1).

▼ Too much emphasis on what was supposed to happen but didn't can distract attention from what actually did happen; people learn more from what they do than from what they don't do.

◆ Detailed attention to objectives may reveal the need to reformulate them; sometimes this will mean making them more specific; sometimes they will need to be expressed in broader terms.

BALANCING OBJECTIVES

In order to set up review topics in advance, agree objectives in these three categories before the activity:

- ACTIVITY OBJECTIVES e.g. to get the whole group from A to B;
- GROUP OBJECTIVES e.g. to involve everyone in decision-making;
- INDIVIDUAL OBJECTIVES e.g. to carry out individual responsibilities.

The last two categories help to make connections between personal and social development more explicit. During the review it is often productive to discuss the extent to which the objectives support or conflict with each other. The balancing of task, team and individual needs is the basis of John Adair's model of Action-Centred Leadership.

ARROWS (1)

> Ask young people to experiment with drawing different kinds of arrows to illustrate objectives and what can happen to them (they can grow, split, fade; be frustrated, diverted, forgotten; shared, supported, achieved etc.). Now ask participants to use some of these arrows to draw a 'prediction picture' of what will happen to their objectives during the next activity.

> After the activity, refer back to these pictures and ask participants to draw what actually happened, using 'artistic arrows'.

ARROWS (2)

> For a more 'scientific' alternative ask participants to draw in the centre of a blank poster a large arrow which shows their main objectives for the activity.

> Now ask them to draw (and label) smaller arrows alongside pointing in the same direction. These smaller arrows represent 'supporting objectives' - examples of what they can do to improve their chances of achieving their main objective.

> Ask them to illustrate any factors (internal or external) which might get in the way with arrows pointing in the opposite direction.

> Ask them to record potential follow-up objectives beyond the arrow. These show what achievement of the main objective will enable them to do more easily and what other 'pay-offs' there might be.

GRIDS

More 'scientific' again is this informative variation on ticking boxes which produces a miniature bar graph for each activity.

> Ask individuals to list their objectives (and any supporting objectives) on squared paper, roughly in order of importance to themselves, leaving space for about eight columns of squares to the right of the list.

> After each activity, ask individuals fill in a square to show which objectives they have achieved. If an objective is only partly achieved, the square is filled in by a corresponding amount.

> See CARDS, POSITIONS and SCORES for alternative ways of monitoring objectives and creating talking points.

OBSERVING group activities and reporting back these observations can heighten awareness of self, of others and of group dynamics.

These two pages are mostly concerned with 'low technology' observation, using paper and pencil. (Refer to VIDEO and TAPE-RECORDING for high technology variations.)

◆ The observer role is very powerful especially if it brings attention to behaviour that is not usually commented on. If, for example, observers are asked only to describe what they see as 'positive' behaviour, this can transform groups where young people (or staff) are quick to criticise but rarely give praise.

INTRODUCING OBSERVATION

OBSERVATION PROJECT: This introduces observation through a group project which requires everyone to be observers at the same time.

> Announce that the group are going to take part in an 'observation project' (of about half an hour). Avoid directing their attention towards anything in particular, but inform them that there will be an 'observation quiz' afterwards. Almost any group activity could be suitable, but a short hill walk is ideal because there are both changing group dynamics and changing surroundings to observe.

> At the top of the hill, or when the activity has finished, ask "What did you observe?" Allow each person to give one answer, and keep the ROUND going (several times if necessary) until there are no more observations forthcoming. Prompt observations about self and each other if this does not happen naturally.

> Finish with a discussion about the value of observing and the value of feeding back observations when learning from experience.

OBSERVING BLINDFOLDED PEOPLE: A fun way of introducing observation is to ask an observer to watch a group blindfold activity. It is interesting for the observer, and it has an obvious purpose; participants are interested to hear from the observer about what they could not see at the time. However, this method does not readily give everyone a chance to experience observing and reporting back.

REPORTING OBSERVATIONS

Rather than starting a review with a report back from an observer (who may well be telling people things they already know, or don't want to know), it is better to start with participants commenting on their performance as a group, after which they can then ask the observer specific questions. But there is a risk that the observer will have little or nothing to add to what the participants have noticed themselves. This risk is minimised if the observer has been asked to notice just one key aspect. It is usually best if the group does not know exactly what is being observed. (An exception is JOGGER CARDS.) Here are some examples of what an observer may be asked to do:

POSITIVES: Identify one positive contribution made by each person.
IDEAS: Record how many ideas each person comes up with, and what happens to these ideas.
DECISIONS: Notice what decisions are made, and how they are made.
SUPPORT: Make a note of the ways people co-operate, help or support each other.
QUOTES: Write down interesting quotes, especially if they do not appear to be heard by everyone.
DIAGRAMS: Sketch diagrams or pictures to show people's positions at different stages of the activity.
SOCIOGRAM: Show each person's position on a bird's eye view diagram, and draw lines from speakers towards the people they are speaking to. Do this for a period of about 3 minutes. This shows patterns of interactions at a glance. These can be produced at intervals throughout an activity.
HAPPY CHART: Sketch a HAPPY CHART to show what changes in group mood were noticed from the perspective of the observer.
TIMES: Record the time by each comment. A group will often be surprised to learn just how much (or how little) time passed during certain stages of the activity.

- Some observation methods may be best carried out by the reviewer, but young people are likely to learn more and become more aware if the role of observer is open to all.

'PERFORMING' describes how (without training in drama skills) young people can create and produce a play for performing to an audience. In the examples below, the performance is based on a theme which allows young people to draw on their experiences of learning through doing. Ideally, the performance also anticipates the future application of what has been learned. Neither example depends on the reviewer being able to provide training in drama skills - nor do these examples depend on young people having acting talents. However, the examples below do assume that the young people involved have already demonstrated that they have sufficient motivation and groupwork skills to tackle independent tasks successfully. (Also refer to 'PRESENTATIONS'.)

A PERFORMANCE BASED ON ACTION REPLAYS

If the group members enjoyed doing an ACTION REPLAY (or another drama-based reviewing method), they may feel more confident building on their existing achievement than starting from scratch. These are some questions to ask a group thinking about converting an action replay into a performance in front of an audience:

- *What do you think the audience reaction to your original action replay would have been? What would they have made of it?*
- *As a piece of 'theatre', what was really good about the first time you did it? How can you keep (and build on) these good points?*
- *What could you leave out from the first time that wouldn't be missed?*
- *What else do you want to communicate to the audience that does not come across through action replay? How can you communicate these things? (Don't keep exclusively to action replay: think about mixing action replay with other kinds or styles of performance.)*
- *Are you going to include playing with the controls (pause, reverse, fast forward, etc.) in the performance? If so, why?*
- *What messages do you want to get across?*
- *How will you judge your success afterwards?*

YOUTH EMPOWERMENT: TURNING IDEAS INTO ACTION

This page describes how two performances were set up during a weekend of activity-based learning for young people from Clydebank. (The programme had included physical, creative, and problem-solving activities.)

GETTING IDEAS TOGETHER: As an introduction to 'brainstorming', small groups listed 'all' the possible uses of a stone, then selected what they felt were their best and most original ideas.

This was followed by a 'brainstorm' about 'power' and a five minute performance about 'power'. It was felt that the pace of this exercise would help groups to get over any fears about performing, so that these would not get in the way of the main performance later in the day. (The group which found this most difficult chose to make a video for the main 'performance' project.)

POWER: This was the written briefing for the first performance.

"A challenge against the clock! Your group has 15 minutes to get ideas and prepare for a 5 minute play about POWER. Everyone in the group must come up with an idea of their own before the group decides which idea (or ideas) to use. Everyone in the group should have an important part in the play. You can choose any site for your play that is within one minute's walk from the main meeting room, provided that twenty people will be able to see and hear the action."

IDEAS INTO ACTION: the written briefing for the main performance.

"You have been practising the skills needed for 'IDEAS INTO ACTION' - teamwork, getting ideas, making decisions, performing as a group. This is your chance to bring it all together into a 20 minute production.

You are free to use any issues, themes, ideas, media or skills from the weekend so far, but your production should include:

- everyone in your group playing an important part in the preparation and the performance;

- a positive picture of the future for young people in Clydebank;

- some ideas about how this positive picture was achieved;

- a message. [9]

PICTURES can be used at all stages of reviewing with individuals or groups. They can help people to show what they were doing, seeing, thinking or feeling.

▲ Pictures expand the 'language' of reviewing and open up new channels of communication. Some people find it easier to think and express themselves through pictures; many find it easier to talk when they can refer to a picture as a visual aid.

▼ Unfortunately there are others who are resistant, believing they cannot draw. The skill in using pictures as a reviewing aid is in using methods which minimise this negative view.

◆ 'Non-artists' can use pictures by:
choosing a ready-made picture; making a collage; taking photographs and talking about them; giving instructions to someone else to draw the picture in their minds; or producing 'abstract art' in which there is no expectation of creating realistic likenesses.

◆ In a supportive learning climate, even young people who think they cannot draw may take the risk and discover they can!

CHOOSE A PICTURE

The reviewer will need a varied and stimulating collection of pictures (including abstract ones). Providing an assortment of magazines is the easiest option; a better one is for the reviewer to build up one or two picture scrapbooks of their own, or an interesting collection of postcards.

> Ask individuals to choose a picture which represents one or more of the following:

something important about your experience; your best experience; your worst experience; what you wish it had been like; your part in the activity; what the group was like; your hopes for the next activity.

> Ask them either to explain their choice or to ask others to guess.

◆ The whole group can be asked to choose just one picture to represent a group theme such as 'what the group was like'.

◆ If individuals can't find a picture, they can be given the option of altering one, or drawing or describing one.

MAKE A COLLAGE

A collage is itself a 'picture' (which can include other pictures within it). It can be made from almost any materials that can be stuck onto a sheet of paper. The reviewer can supply an interesting variety of materials, or can ask the group to search for suitable material during or after the activity (whether indoors or outdoors).
> Individuals are asked to find (say) three items which they want to include in a group collage about the activity.
> The group meet and individuals explain why they want to include each of their three items.
> The group are given (say) 10 minutes' planning time to decide on an outline design for the collage and to decide who does what.
> After planning, the group have (say) 20 minutes to complete the collage.

- ◆ Unlike SKETCH MAP or CARTOONS, a collage need not be presented in chronological order. Other ways of organising material can be adopted.
- ◆ If there is too much conflict or redundancy for a whole group exercise, then individuals or subgroups can make collages.

DRAW OR PAINT A PICTURE

If young people *are* asked to draw or paint, what styles and subjects are most suitable? Realistic drawings are generally the most difficult to produce and the least useful for reviewing. For most reviewing purposes, abstract pictures are preferable, whether using expressionistic finger-painting, deliberate symbolism, or flow diagrams. Abstract pictures are easier to produce, are likely to be better talking points and, because abstract pictures are more 'context-free', any learning is likely to have a wider relevance.
BEFORE AND AFTER: Before an activity participants draw their expectations, or hopes and fears; afterwards they draw what happened. Pictures are compared and discussed.
PROBLEMS AND ACHIEVEMENTS: Individuals draw one picture representing group problems during the activity and another representing group achievements. The whole group then produces pictures on the same subjects, incorporating ideas from each individual's drawing.
For more ideas see *Art Therapy for Groups* by Marian Liebmann. [10]

When playing back a video or audio recording there are several ways in which it can be used for reviewing. These are some of the options:

PLAYBACK 1: CHARTS

> Everyone is asked to make individual HAPPY CHARTS during the playback.

> The recording is played back with about 10 pauses. At each pause, each person marks a cross on their graph.

> The completed charts are compared and discussed. They can also be redrawn onto a giant HAPPY CHART to see what other patterns appear.

> It is possible to chart themes other than happiness such as confidence, effort, influence, motivation etc.

PLAYBACK 2: QUESTIONS

> During the playback, press the pause button every minute or two, or whenever requested to do so.

> Ask everyone to write down questions each time the playback is paused:

- *"Questions you actually asked at the time."*
- *"Questions in your mind at the time."*
- *"Questions you would like to ask now - to anyone or everyone."*

> Everyone reads out their questions while you quickly note down the subject of each question on a poster.

> Repeat this process for each pause, starting a new poster each time. (The sequence of posters produces an interesting profile of the activity and there will also be plenty of questions to discuss!)

PLAYBACK 3: CHANGES

> During the playback, anyone can request a 'pause'.

> The individual requesting the pause now proposes something they would like to have changed:

- *"I wish I had ..."*
- *"I wish you had ..."*
- *"It would have been better if ..."*

PLAYBACK 4: SOUNDS

- REPORT: A dummy microphone is passed round in turn while a video is played back *without the sound.* The holder of the microphone provides a 'voice-over' commentary on the action in the style of a news reporter or sports commentator
- THINKING ALOUD: whoever is on-screen is passed the 'microphone' and speaks aloud what they were thinking at the time.
- MISSING SOUNDS: the viewers provide the missing sounds and words.

PLAYBACK 5: SIGHTS

> Before playing back the audiotape (or video soundtrack) explain that "the picture has been lost", and you are asking the group to provide the 'silent film' to go with the soundtrack.
> A space for ACTION REPLAY is cleared; explain that no props are to be used.
> Replay the audio-tape (or video soundtrack) so that the group can re-enact what happened, synchronised with the soundtrack.

PLAYBACK 6: BRIEFING

> If there is a verbal briefing of about 10 minutes before a particularly special or challenging activity, then record it!
> During the review, play back this recording, pausing it every minute (or when requested), and ask each person to recall what they were thinking or feeling at the time.

PLAYBACK 7: STATEMENTS

> Before the activity, each person records a brief statement about their hopes, fears, expectations, responsibilities, predictions etc.
> These recordings are played back after the activity. (This is less formal and more dramatic than referring to written statements).

PLAYBACK 8: INCIDENTS

> If a key incident has been captured on film, then everyone is given the opportunity to provide a commentary during the playback or to explain what they were doing or thinking at the time.

Individuals show their POSITION (point of view) by their POSITION (place) on a giant 'map'. In its simplest form, the 'map' is a single spectrum with each end representing opposing points of view.

There are many metaphorical phrases in which points of view are described in terms of physical space, such as: 'poles apart', 'at opposite ends of a spectrum'; 'where I stand on this issue', 'where I draw the line', 'making my position clear'; 'sharing common ground', etc.. Such connections between opinion and place should suggest a number of possibilities for active reviewing. Here is a start ...

LINE-UPS ABOUT GROUP BEHAVIOUR

Participants arrange themselves along an imaginary line which represents a spectrum of viewpoints on the chosen topic. Mark out a curved line (e.g. using a rope) so that everyone can see each other.
EXAMPLES:

1) How much CARING do you think there was towards each other? One end represents 'too much caring'; the other 'not enough caring'.
2) How much GROUP EFFORT went into achieving the task? One end represents 'the maximum possible'; the other 'not very much'.
3) To what extent was this GROUP ACTION POINT achieved? (e.g. 'to include everyone in decisions') One end represents 100%; the other 0%.

◆ Discussing their position with neighbours in a 'line-up' will help individuals lacking confidence to express their points of view - because they will probably find themselves talking to the person in the group who is most likely to support their own point of view.

LINE-UPS ABOUT INDIVIDUAL BEHAVIOUR

1) Who TALKED MOST? Who TALKED LEAST? ... Arrange yourselves in a spectrum between these two people ... If you are happy with the amount of talking you did, stay where you are. If you would rather be somewhere else on this spectrum, then move to that place.
2) How much do you think you ENCOURAGED OTHERS? (a lot - not a lot)
3) How many IDEAS did you contribute? (a lot - not a lot)
4) How OBSERVANT do you think you were? (very - not very)

TWO DIMENSIONAL LINE-UPS

These are particularly valuable where objectives are partly in conflict during an activity - and a balance has to be found. For example, team objectives and individual objectives sometimes support each other and sometimes compete with each other.

EXAMPLES:

1) How much effort did you put into achieving your INDIVIDUAL OBJECTIVES? (One side of a square represents 100% effort at one end; 0% effort at the other.) How much effort did you put into achieving TEAM OBJECTIVES? (Facing the opposite side of the square, people stay put for an answer of 0%, moving as far as the opposite side if they think they put 100% effort into achieving team objectives.)
2) How much did you ENJOY the activity? (show this on dimension 1) How do you rate your ACHIEVEMENT? (dimension 2)
3) How much did others LISTEN TO YOU during the activity? (show this on dimension 1) How much did you LISTEN TO OTHERS? (dimension 2)

▲ These methods introduce new talking points and ...
- check or correct assumptions about group opinion;
- help to refocus or revitalise a meandering discussion;
- help people to state their position clearly - especially useful if they are confused, inconsistent, or are not readily speaking up;
- give individuals the chance to reconsider their position;
- can provide a before-and-after measure to see how opinions have changed during a discussion (if at all);
- help a group to discover whether they are arguing about 'nothing' (points of view may turn out to be much closer than was apparent);
- help a group to pinpoint differences and work out compromises.

▼ Not all issues can be neatly represented in terms of a point on a scale, or a place on a map - so, once they are in place, encourage people to express any qualifications they wish to make.

◆ Where there are more than two issues to consider at the same time these can be represented by objects or words placed at different points in the room. Individuals take it in turns to walk a route on this 'map' which represents their 'journey' during the activity - showing how their attention moved from one issue to another.

PREDICTION exercises set up fascinating reviews.
Some examples of the potential of prediction work are described below; other examples are described in SCORES.

FIRST IMPRESSIONS

> Look around at everyone else in the group, and just think ...
- Can you remember what your first impressions of them were?
- Do you have any idea of what their first impressions of you were?

> Try to forget your current impressions of each other, and go back to the first impressions you can remember, and write them down.
> Try to guess what others have written about you, and write these down.
> Before talking about your impressions, put a score by each person's name on your list. Score 0 if your first impressions are exactly the same as your current impressions. Mark down a plus score (any number up to 5) if the person has since gone up in your estimation. Mark down a minus score (any number down to minus 5) if the person has since gone down in your estimation.
> Now invite discussion:
- How accurate were your first impressions?
- Why were your first impressions not more accurate?
- What particular things have others done that have made them go up or down in your estimation?
- How accurate were your guesses about what others had written about their first impressions of you?

> Finish with a ROUND for each person: "What you have done that has impressed me most is ..."

PREDICTIONS ABOUT SELF

People with low self-esteem underestimate their capabilities. The strategy of setting small achievable objectives to build up confidence is described in OBJECTIVES. This contrasting strategy can be equally effective for enhancing self-esteem:
> Before an activity, ask people to predict their feelings, their behaviour and their achievements.
> After the activity, ask people to compare their predictions with what actually happened (the likely answer being "better than predicted")

◆ If it turns out that individuals are over-confident and tend to over-estimate their ability, this exercise still serves a useful (if different) purpose. Whatever their level of self-esteem, this exercise will increase young people's self-awareness.

PREDICTIONS ABOUT OTHERS

> Before an activity everyone secretly records personal predictions such as:

- about what will happen (e.g. motivation, enjoyment or success);
- about group behaviour (e.g. teamwork, co-operation, competitiveness);
- about how each individual will behave (e.g. leader, joker, skiver).

> Alternatives:

- predictions can be discussed and recorded in pairs;
- predictions can be drawn as pictures or diagrams (especially those relating to the group as a whole);
- predictions can be recorded on tape.

> Before the activity starts (especially if it is an independent activity in which safety is a concern), ask if anyone has predicted an accident! Discussion of such concerns can only improve safety; all other discussion can wait until the review.

▲ Making predictions is a test of how well people know each other. It is also a useful preparation exercise: it is a mental rehearsal of what might happen during the activity, and it anticipates review issues.

The psychology of secret predictions is fascinating. For example, they tend to prevent disruptive or unhelpful behaviour during an activity; if this happens discuss the reason during the review.

▼ If over-used or over-emphasised, participants think more about predictions than anything else: other objectives are more important.

◆ It is interesting to finish prediction exercises with a discussion about situations in which it is and is not good to be unpredictable.

Some reviewing methods need to be set up well in advance, involving PREPARATION before the programme or before the activity.

Planning reviewing into a programme before the activities are decided is the ultimate in preparation!

PRACTISING USEFUL SKILLS

For some reviewing methods it is useful for young people to practise specific skills beforehand such as drama skills, observation skills, video-recording, tape-recording, photography, etc.

VARYING REVIEWING METHODS

Although a reviewer may have a favourite style or method of reviewing, this may not be the best way for each young person to learn. Just as some people will get more from some activities than others, so some people will get more from some reviewing methods than others. Planning to use a wide variety of reviewing methods means that everyone will be learning for most of the time. Variety will also add interest and motivation (for all), and will continually open up new perspectives.

SEQUENCING REVIEWING METHODS

> To plan a reviewing sequence for a programme, list the objectives and supporting objectives, and arrange them in a logical sequence.

> On one side of each objective write down potential reviewing methods. On the other side of each objective, write down the activities that are most likely to precede these reviews.

> When presenting or negotiating the programme, ensure that the objectives (or themes) for each session of the programme are the most prominent feature.

> If young people are keen to do a particular activity, then they first have to work out if, where and how it can fit into the planned 'thematic' sequence, such as: awareness ➜ trust ➜ support ➜ achievement ➜ feedback ➜ action planning.

PREPARATION BY YOUNG PEOPLE

> Before the activity, ask the group to list potential review topics, and ask each individual (or pair) to take responsibility for leading a topic during the review. (Allow up to half of the group to postpone their choice until after the activity.)

> When all have decided on a topic give them time to prepare. The reviewer is available for advice during preparation, but is involved as little as possible during the review itself.

▲ Young people will often respond well when their friends are leading the review. This is even more the case when they know that they will all have a turn at leading a review topic.

▼ If the reviewer gets too involved after delegating responsibility, the advantages of this method are soon lost.

◆ Leading a review topic can be a greater responsibility or challenge than the activity being reviewed - so ensure that all reviewers receive feedback on how they conducted their part of the review.

PREPARING THE REVIEW (BUT NOT THE ACTIVITY)

It is not always necessary to determine the activity: it can be sufficient simply to agree the agenda for reviewing. For example, a group is left in an interesting location for a specified time, with agreed review topics (for later) but without an activity. The location can be anywhere from a small empty island (requiring imagination) to a busy amusement park (requiring choice). The review topics might be:

- high points and low points;
- what was strange or interesting;
- decisions made during this time;
- the extent to which objectives were achieved.

◆ Agreeing a review structure in advance of an otherwise unstructured experience helps young people to make productive use of their time - and it makes for an interesting review which young people are well prepared for.

PRESENTATIONS are opportunities for young people to communicate to others about their experiences and what they have learned. They are an excellent way of reviewing expeditions.

GETTING THE MESSAGE ACROSS

Presentations are sometimes contained *within* an activity - with one group (or subgroup) presenting its experiences to another group (or subgroup). Presentations *at the end of an activity* are likely to be more 'public', especially if the audience includes people who have not been part of the experience. The course might be 'on show' and this is the audience's way of finding out what it was all about.

▲ Communicating to others about an activity-based programme is yet another opportunity for learning; it involves looking at the whole experience from a new point of view, and 're-viewing' the course from an 'outside' perspective. It is also a chance for re-inforcing the central theme or purpose of a programme.

CONVERTING REVIEWING METHODS

How do young people explain to outsiders what it was like, what they have got from it, and what they have learned? These are the $64,000 questions! It is notoriously difficult for people (of any age) to communicate about significant personal experiences without being stuck for words or resorting to cliché. But these questions are not quite so difficult to answer, if the young people have been in the habit of reviewing their experiences. If the reviewing has included creative and dramatic methods, there should be plenty of ideas (and perhaps even ready-made resources) for ways in which young people can communicate their experiences to outsiders. Although most reviewing methods described in this book have no audience in mind, many of the methods can be readily converted to form part of a presentation.

CONFIDENTIALITY: If any material was produced solely for the purpose of reviewing, and is now being considered as part of a presentation, ensure that the producers of this material (video, writing, art work) have given their full consent for it to be used for this new purpose.

SOMETHING TO SHOW

Having something to show helps young people to communicate to others about the experience. It is in everyone's interests (providers, participants, audience and other stakeholders) to ensure that presentations (in whatever form) are well prepared and do justice to the programme. How young people present what they have been doing and learning to others is an issue which is best considered *before* a programme starts. Should it be formal or informal? Should it be in the form of group or individual presentations or both? Messages about the experience can be presented in the following ways:

> *logbooks, reports, portfolios, photograph album, slide show, video, exhibition, open evening, play, demonstration of skills, ceremony, discussion, meeting, campaign, article in a local newspaper, personal souvenirs, artwork, music, etc.*

SPREADING THE GOOD NEWS

When reviewers are working hard to encourage young people to express themselves *within* a group, it can too easily happen that the subject of communicating with *outsiders* about their experiences becomes an afterthought. It can be vitally important for influential people in a young person's life to be faced with the good news about them - especially if their restricted or prejudiced view has not yet allowed them to see the young person's true capabilities. If the experience was 'good news', then the more people who know about it, the more chance there is that the young person will discover that they are living in a favourable world in which their talents and their better nature are recognised. This is particularly important for young people who are stuck with reputations or 'labels' that they are trying hard to leave behind.

IF ONLY MY MUM COULD SEE ME NOW!

- *Who would have been most surprised to have seen what you have been doing - and why?*
- *What would you like them to know?*
- *What is the best way of letting them know?*

QUESTIONNAIRES can be used at any stage of a reviewing sequence ...

▲ They can help to clarify facts. They can provide a record of the experience. They can open up new ways of looking at experiences. They can help young people to organise their thoughts, and to work out ideas for follow-up and future action.

◆ Questionnaires can also have *administrative* functions at the beginning and end of courses - to clarify objectives and to provide feedback to course organisers - but neither of these functions is primarily a *reviewing* one. These two pages outline a variety of ways in which questionnaires can be used as a *reviewing* method.

QUICK QUESTIONNAIRES

An example of this method can be found in LEARNING TO LEARN (REVIEWING TO DEVELOP LEARNING SKILLS) where the same questionnaire is completed at the end of every skiing session, and is then used as a prompt for discussion in pairs. The ticking and scoring of ten items takes only a minute or two, and its simplicity means that comparisons are readily made between different people's questionnaires or between the same person's questionniares over several sessions. This is also an example of a questionnaire which focuses exclusively on one aspect of the experience - in this case on learning skills.

INDIVIDUALISED QUESTIONNAIRES

Each person completes a unique questionnaire which is tailored to their own interests, strengths, weaknesses, objectives etc. Here are two examples of how individualised questionnaires can be produced:

1) After the activity, each person signs a blank piece of paper and passes it to the left. The recipient writes down a question (relating to the signatory's part in the activity) and passes the paper on, until eventually it arrives back at its starting point. (To save duplication, ask participants to read preceding questions before writing their own).

2) Before the activity, each person creates their own questionnaire, about their interests, targets, action points, responsibilities etc.

TAILOR-MADE QUESTIONNAIRES

These are specific to the experiences of a particular group. It is natural to 'tailor' questions for ROUNDS or for GUIDED REFLECTION; the same can be done for questionnaires. If a photocopier or a word processor is available, tailor-made questionnaires can be readily produced.

▲ This approach is particularly useful:
- when short of time for a group review;
- if the group is too large for group reviewing methods;
- or if it is believed that the completion of individual questionnaires will be good preparation for a group discussion.

QUESTIONNAIRES FOR NOTE-TAKING

Short review breaks are provided during the activity for individuals to make notes in answer to a few questions. The questions may be standard ones which provide a structure for note-taking, or the reviewer may decide on questions which arise directly from what has been happening since the last break.

QUESTIONS BASED ON SKILLS CHECKLISTS

Lists of personal and social competencies (like the one shown) can be used as checklists for self-assessment. Such lists can be adapted for reviewing activities by asking young people to choose three skills which they feel they used well, and three skills which they wish they had used, or had used more effectively.

Skill %
STARTING A CONVERSATION
CARRYING ON A CONVERSATION
ENDING A CONVERSATION
LISTENING
EXPRESSING A COMPLIMENT
EXPRESSING APPRECIATION
EXPRESSING ENCOURAGEMENT
ASKING FOR HELP
GIVING INSTRUCTIONS
EXPRESSING AFFECTION
EXPRESSING A COMPLAINT
PERSUADING OTHERS
EXPRESSING ANGER
RESPONDING TO PRAISE
RESPONDING TO THE FEELINGS OF OTHERS
APOLOGISING
FOLLOWING INSTRUCTIONS
RESPONDING TO PERSUASION
RESPONDING TO FAILURE
RESPONDING TO CONTRADICTORY MESSAGES
RESPONDING TO A COMPLAINT
RESPONDING TO ANGER
SETTING A GOAL
GATHERING INFORMATION
CONCENTRATING ON A TASK
EVALUATING YOUR ABILITIES
PREPARING FOR A STRESSFUL CONVERSATION
SETTING PROBLEM PRIORITIES
DECISION-MAKING
RECOGNISING WHICH EMOTION YOU ARE FEELING
DETERMINING RESPONSIBILITY
MAKING REQUESTS
RELAXATION
SELF-CONTROL
NEGOTIATION
HELPING OTHERS
ASSERTIVENESS

(An extract from material produced by the Scottish Intermediate Treatment Resource Centre.)

QUESTIONS

Asking the group QUESTIONS is a popular form of reviewing - more popular than it should be, because it is often used when little thought has been given to alternative methods.

The skilled reviewer needs to be skilled in the art of questioning, but many young people find it difficult to respond to even the most carefully thought out question when there is a group audience listening to their every word. Many of the methods in this book aim to create less intimidating settings which allow young people time to think, and provide a variety of ways in which they can express themselves.

◆ By creating the situation (and learning climate) in which young people can most readily answer, reviewers are at least half-way to becoming skilled in the art of questioning.

QUESTIONS ON A THEME

Suitable themes to explore through questioning are: *communicating effectively, being assertive, co-operating, deciding, listening, planning, making friends, solving problems, being creative, thinking positively, achievement etc*. The theme may have been designed into the activity, or it may have emerged during the activity. These are some of the questions a reviewer might ask, having decided to focus on a particular theme ('x') and to do so by asking questions which follow the REVIEWING SEQUENCE described on page 13:

1) EXPERIENCE: What were the main examples of x happening during the activity? What were the main examples of x not happening?
2) EXPRESS: What feelings do you associate with each of these examples? What was it like to be involved (or not involved) in x?
3) EXAMINE: Which four examples are most different from each other? What was PLUS, MINUS and INTERESTING about each event? What were the causes and consequences of each event?
4) EXPLORE: What is the next step you will take (individually and as a group) to improve on x?

◆ If curiosity and creativity is to be encouraged, then young people should also be providing review questions.

TRIGGER QUESTIONS

When questions are simply trigger questions, it is not important to get a direct answer: what matters most is that a trigger (whether coaxing or provocative) stimulates discussion. Closed evaluative questions (*"Was it good?" "Would you do it again?"*) are notoriously poor triggers. More effective questions for starting a discussion are open questions about facts and feelings (*"What did you do when ...?"* or *"How did it feel when ...?"*)

◆ Trigger questions are also a useful search technique for bringing out issues that can be examined and explored later.

ANALYTICAL QUESTIONING

Analytical questioning can help young people to analyse a problem faced during an activity. In the purest form of this method, the reviewer provides no ideas or opinions, but simply helps participants to think in a more disciplined way *using participants' own language.* This method first involves examining one word or one phrase at a time. If, for example, the problem was stated as "WE COULDN'T DECIDE WHAT TO DO", ask:

- Did you have some ideas about WHAT TO DO? If so, what were they?
- WE? *Who* exactly was trying to decide (and how much)?
- What did trying to DECIDE involve? (What did it look/sound like?)
- What exactly do you mean by "COULDN'T"? (How hard did you try?)

> Now ask the group to see if they can produce a more accurate version of the original statement (making use of the answers given).

> Now identify (and map) the various FORCES involved by asking:

- What was preventing you from deciding? (Identify various blocks)
- Had you made a decision, what would have been the benefits?
- What were the benefits in not deciding what to do?

▲ This sequence of questioning should result in a clearer statement of the problem (together with a diagram of the forces involved).

▼ It could be too late after the activity for it to be worth examining the problem in such detail - unless the problem is a recurring one.

◆ A more practical application of analytical questioning is to use it for a MID-ACTIVITY REVIEW when a group are 'stuck' during an activity.

REPEATING THE ACTIVITY provides three opportunities for reviewing ...

BEFORE	REPLANNING: reviewing the activity in preparation for repeating it (with or without changes to the activity).
DURING	REVIEWING WHILE DOING: making comparisons while doing the activity for a second time.
AFTER	REVIEWING BOTH ACTIVITIES TOGETHER: making comparisons *after* doing the activity for a second time.

REPLANNING BY STAFF

Change whatever you want to bring attention to:
- change who does what (to look at responsibilities or relationships);
- reduce support (to look at independence);
- change or introduce 'rules' about communication (to highlight communication issues);
- agree what people should do if they feel left out (to focus on participation);
- use observers or commentators (to heighten awareness of key issues);
- or simply change the objective (without changing the activity).

REPLANNING BY THE GROUP

Inform the group that there will be x minutes' planning time for a second attempt. Before they start planning, ask individuals (or pairs) to list five things they need to pay attention to if they are to improve second time round. At the end of the planning time, provide feedback on the planning process, and ask the group to predict how well they will do. Check whether they now want to do the activity again, or would prefer to apply what they have learnt to something new. Whichever option they choose, the fact that they were planning for a real and immediate event will have helped to focus energy and attention during the review.

VISIONING THE SECOND ATTEMPT

"How would you have preferred things to turn out? Tell the story (in a ROUND) of how things turned out better the second time." The story can be told first in fantasy style and then in a realistic but optimistic style *as if it had really happened.*

REPEATING WITH COMMENTARY

"Try the activity again, but this time take it in turns to provide a commentary on what is happening. When you are the commentator try to make comparisons with the first attempt whenever you see a chance to do so." The commentator should be encouraged to point out both similarities and differences.

SINGLE ACTIVITY GROUPS

Where a single activity holds a group together, the above strategies will help maximise opportunities for personal and social development, while also developing interest and skill in the activity.

▲ Repeating the activity provides:
- a chance to repeat something enjoyable;
- a chance to improve performance or to put right what was wrong;
- a chance to experience different roles and responsibilities;
- a chance to be more observant and more aware of others;
- a chance to test out an idea, perhaps as a response to someone saying "If only ...", "I could have ...", "We should have ..." etc.
- a fresh perspective from which to look at the first experience.
- a chance to follow 'failure' with a relative success.

▼ Repeating the activity might produce much the same experience and much the same review; or an even worse experience than the first time round. This may not be the outcome wanted, but comparing the two events is still likely to provide a useful review angle.

◆ Criticism that might otherwise be seen as 'picking holes', or 'rubbing salt in the wounds' will be more welcome if participants see it as feedback which will help them do better next time - especially if 'next time' is imminent.

Any of these 'REPORTS' could include statements about what a young person has learned or achieved through taking part in activities:

Record of Achievement, Award Record Book, Record of Experience, Curriculum Vitae, School Report, Social Enquiry Report, Community-Based Assessment, Logbook, Course Report, Certificate, Reference, Competency Statement, Portfolio.

Many readers of such reports will expect to find insights into a young person's development. These two pages provide ideas for producing reports which reflect the true potential of the individual concerned, by ensuring that good news (in particular) is recorded, and that it is presented in a suitable format.

FORMATS

For some purposes, 'a suitable format' might be concise and formal, but more informative approaches (such as a portfolio of items collected during reviews) are also valued in many situations. The format described below is a three-part report comprising SELF APPRAISAL, PEER APPRAISAL and STAFF APPRAISAL. The chief merit of this format is that its several perspectives provide readers with a more complete picture. (Readers can always choose to pay more attention to whichever perspective interests them most). Like the portfolio approach, it can make use of material generated by many of the review methods described in this book.

SELF APPRAISAL: A report should demonstrate that the young person is capable of reflecting on and learning from their experiences. If young people report on their experience *in their own language*, this will often provide greater insight and have more credibility than even the most eloquent statement from staff. A self appraisal can be structured as a series of statements such as: *"What I achieved ... what I experienced ... what I learned ... what I'm beginning to learn."* It could also make use of extracts from a logbook or diary or use items from review sessions. It can include charts, diagrams or other illustrations that have been produced during reviews. It can be set out in the form of an ACTION PLAN or resolutions.

PEER APPRAISAL: Assessment of young people by each other is a particularly effective way of affirming the qualities and abilities brought out through activities. Young people can often provide the most insightful perspective of all for a report. Appraisal comments from others can be recorded and collected during review sessions when feedback is given. If such material is not available, a special session can be set up in which the whole group (or subgroups) generate appraisal comments for each person. Ideally these comments are supported by reference to specific events or situations.

◆ I have found that young people not known for their sensitivity will rise to the occasion when they are taking it in turns as givers and receivers of appraisal, and when they know they are producing a report that could be of special value to some or all of the group.

STAFF APPRAISAL: This could be the smallest section of a report if reviewing has produced plenty of material for the first two sections. Only if young people are unable to say much about themselves or each other will it be necessary for staff to write much more than an endorsement. Even if reviews have not directly produced material for reports, reviewers will at least have a much closer and more rounded knowledge of individuals as a result of regular reviewing.

THE MORE PERSPECTIVES THE BETTER

A ten week community-based assessment programme demonstrated that:

- *the more situations and perspectives that are included (self, other young people, various adults), the greater the impact and credibility of the assessment - to the young person as well as to others;*
- *the more people who are involved in the assessment process, the more likely it is that the young person will find that they are living in a fairer world, and one in which people have woken up to their prejudices and responsibilities towards the young person.* [11]

Increased awareness of ROLES can be highlighted by reviewing the ways in which individuals participate in group activities.

For some young people, there may be no recognisable pattern to their involvement, but for others there will be some fairly consistent patterns of behaviour. Wherever there is an identifiable pattern this can be termed a 'role'. The reviewing methods described in these two pages enable young people to become more aware of patterns in their own behaviour; to experience a variety of different roles; and (through increased role awareness) to work more effectively as a team.

Many kinds of activities (not necessarily drama-based ones) can be used to create a 'different world' within which there are opportunities to experience a greater variety of roles than 'the real world' normally offers. Activities can be seen as a practice ground for potential future roles (or for developing current ones). If activities are to work in this way, *then it is important to review activities in terms of roles.* This section describes three ways of doing so.

ROLE CHECKLIST: Ask the group to make a list of what they will need to do (individually or collectively) to ensure that the next activity will be successful and enjoyable. After the activity, individuals (preferably on their own) arrange the list in order starting with what they spent most time doing. These individual lists are then checked against the group's perception of each individual's role, and any differences are discussed.

▲ Listing roles in this way heightens awareness of them during the activity and sets up a useful resource for reviewing.

▼ Groups may not find it easy to identify roles in this way - in which case an alternative is to work from a ready-made checklist.

◆ It can help to raise self-esteem if young people discover that they have underestimated the value of their own efforts.

MISSING ROLES: The process of creating an imaginary extra group member encourages young people to analyse what their group is lacking, and indicates whether there are any significant roles 'missing' from the group. The imaginary extra person is created by asking, "What kind of new group member would help you to be more successful as a group?". Encourage the group to name, describe, welcome and include this extra person for the next activity. If the idea does not capture their imagination, then abandon it! (You will have at least created a useful list of 'missing roles' to work with.) But if the idea takes off it creates interesting, if unpredictable, reviews.

▲ Having an imaginary character in the group can add a fascinating extra dimension to the review process.

▼ This new group member could turn out to be highly subversive, but ...

◆ ... although imaginary, the character is a real reflection of the group which has created and developed her or him - so what this invisible person 'does' or 'says' needs to be taken fairly seriously. The creators of the character (like writers of soaps) should find a suitable way of writing the character out of the group when no longer needed - perhaps when there are no longer any roles 'missing'.

STAFF ROLES: Another method for identifying missing roles is to ask the group to list the various roles that the reviewer (and any other staff) are performing and that the group would need to 'take over' to operate more independently. It is then discussed and decided how some of these roles can be taken on by young people themselves.

This exercise worked well with a group of young potato growers who were working towards setting up their own business; staff and young people helped each other to list their various roles, and then worked out ways in which young people could take on more responsibility. [12]

◆ This exercise brings the roles of people working with the group under the spotlight. This is useful because, in trying to be helpful, staff can unwittingly reduce opportunities for development by taking on too many roles themselves. By discussing the issue openly, staff will be able to work out more empowering ways of being helpful.

ROUNDS are sentences started by the reviewer and finished by each person in turn. The sentences can be about facts or feelings, self or others, past, present or future.

▲ Rounds introduce some basic principles common to many reviewing methods, such as the right to be heard and the right to pass. Rounds are particularly useful ...
- when everyone has got a lot to say;
- when there is unbalanced participation in a group;
- when searching for a review topic;
- for quickly checking how each person is feeling (or thinking);
- for creating a particular mood (through careful sequencing of rounds).

SENTENCE BEGINNINGS

Rounds can be pitched at any level. By trying out different sentence beginnings, the reviewer can find the level at which people are most willing and able to take part. Amongst the advantages of sentence beginnings over questions are that:
- they require less thinking (half the 'answer' is supplied);
- they usually produce clear statements (full sentence answers);
- their regular repetition helps to keep answers to the point.

EXAMPLES

The high point for me was when ...
The low point for me was when ...
The hardest thing for me was ...
The easiest thing for me was ...
What surprised me was ...
Something I knew would happen was ...
Nobody listened when ...
I'm really pleased that I ...
I wish I had ...
I felt like going home when ...
If I'd had a camera ...
If I could do it again I would ...
I wish I had been asked ...
I was annoyed when ...
My motivation went down when ...
My motivation went up when ...
I was helped by ...

I helped ...
I appreciated ...
I was appreciated by ...
I'd like to complain to ...
I'd like to congratulate ...
I'd like the group to tell me ...
One last thing I'd like to say is ...

SOME USEFUL SEQUENCES AND COMBINATIONS
EXPRESSION: What I found difficult/easy/interesting/satisfying ...
FEEDBACK: I felt ... when you ... (One round about each person)
LEARNING: What I learned ... What I'm beginning to learn is ...
PLANNING: If only ... Next time ...
CLOSING: I'd like to thank/apologise to/congratulate ...

VARIATIONS
CARDS: During the activity, you were the person who ... (see CARDS).
THREE WORDS: Each person sums up the experience in three words.
ORBITS: Rounds are started by group members - who will effectively be setting the 'agenda' for each round.
MIME: Sentence beginnings are completed by mime - which can sometimes be easier than finding the right words!

▼ People may not listen well if they are too anxious about what they will say for their turn. This pressure can be reduced by:
- allowing time for thinking or making notes before a round starts;
- allowing passing, or repetition of what someone else has said;
- starting with different people for each round.

▼ Rounds can be overused with the result that the routine stifles discussion rather than stimulates it. [13]

These three exercises show how SCORES can be used for the prediction and assessment of performance against personal or group goals.

▲ Scoring is a very flexible reviewing aid which is simple and quick, and which can be readily displayed in graphs or diagrams.

▼ When using any scoring system, care needs to be taken that it is used in a way that is compatible with other reviewing strategies - and does not suddenly destroy the learning climate!

◆ Scoring can be made to fit *any* philosophy - much depending on who decides what is to be scored; who does the scoring; and on how the scores are reviewed. Scoring on its own would be a very crude reviewing method, but it is remarkable how numbers focus attention, bring out issues and open the door to more in-depth reviewing.

GOAL SCORES: PREDICTING SCORES FOR SELF AND GROUP

> *Before* an activity, individuals record their private predictions about the extent to which their personal goals will be achieved. They predict their score out of ten for (say): personal enjoyment; personal achievement; co-operation with others; and any specific personal goal.

> Individuals are now asked to predict how many points out of ten the *group* will deserve for (say): motivation; keeping to ground rules; finishing on time; and achieving any specific group goal.

> *After* the activity, individuals record (next to their predicted scores) the scores they think they and the group deserve.

> They then report to the group on the relative differences between each pair of scores, e.g. *"I enjoyed it more than I thought I would, but I didn't co-operate with others as much as I hoped ... The biggest difference was 'group motivation': it was far higher than I expected."*

BETTING: PREDICTING INDIVIDUAL PERFORMANCE

Before doing a *brand new* activity (for which there is no previous 'form' on which to base predictions) individuals estimate how well everyone (including themselves) will perform. The scoring system is explained: *"Those who achieve this standard will earn 10 points, 9 points if they achieve this standard etc."* The main purpose of making predictions is so that the reasoning behind them can now be examined ...

- MAGES

SELF-IMAGES are anything that people make to represent themselves. As a reviewing method, SELF-IMAGES are more specific: "This is me *doing the activity*!".

If time allows, individuals can produce a series of images each representing a different stage of the activity. Images can be in the form of life-size drawings, collages, diagrams, finger painting, junk statues, or any form of modelling using natural, junk or art materials.

- ▲ New methods of self-expression help people think in new ways about themselves.
- ▲ Making things that represent self provides people with the time and opportunity for reflecting about themselves in some depth.
- ▲ There is much to be gained from making the image and from the informal discussion that is likely to accompany this process.
- ▲ It is valuable to follow the making process with discussion and feedback based on the images produced; self-images can generate more perceptive feedback and discussion than would arise from talk alone.

- ▼ The minus side of people getting really involved is that they can feel hurt if their creations are interfered with in a joking or malicious way - so obtain agreement beforehand about what should and should not be done with other people's creations. Because of the high personal investment in constructed self-images (even apparently unwanted ones), it is important that it is the creator who disposes of them (unless taking them away as a souvenir).

- ◆ It is generally easier to give, accept or reject feedback when it is provided through a symbol.

- ◆ If the images are displayed, they are likely to inspire plenty of informal appraisal. [14]

MODELLING

Individuals mould clay (or other material) to represent their own experience in the group, or their experience of a recent activity. Others then interpret the model. The modeller offers an explanation if they want to.

Alternatively, after creating their image, individuals can privately record what it signifies (by recording on tape, or by confiding in a partner). Everyone (in turn) attempts to interpret the image of every other group member (unaided by the person or their partner). The recorded descriptions are then played back or reported by partners.

◆ Making clay self-images was one of the most successful activities in one youth social work group. All the parents commented on it; self-image became a popular talking point. [15]

PERSONAL ACTIVITY MAP

The map is a diagrammatic self-image which, like other self-images, provides interesting talking points.

> As a memory jogger, the group list all of the activities they have done in the group so far, and then add any other activities which any individual particularly likes or dislikes.

> Each person draws a large oval representing a top view of their head, and draws a line dividing the left and right hand sides.

> Using the left hand side (representing past experience), each person writes (or draws) the activities they like most at the front of their 'heads', and the ones they like least at the back.

> On the right hand side, are written (or drawn) activities which individuals have not yet experienced, with the activities they want to try at the front of their 'heads', and the ones they don't want to try at the back.

◆ Personal activity maps probably show far more about a person than simply their views about activities, making it a relatively non-threatening way of exploring self-image. These maps can also suggest activity-based routes for improving self-image.

Producing a SKETCH MAP is a useful starting point for reviewing an expedition, especially if the reviewer was not on the journey.

- ▲ It encourages the group to retrace their route and to relive the experience.
- ▲ It is an efficient way of informing a reviewer about key events and key issues.
- ▲ It is a highly participative reviewing method.
- ▲ Informal reviewing is likely to take place while the map is being made.
- ▲ The end-product is likely to be a useful 'conversation-piece'.
- ▲ It can even be aesthetically pleasing!

MAKING THE SKETCH MAP

> The group is asked to produce one large sketch map (large enough for all the group to work on it together). The map should show:
- where they went;
- what they saw;
- what they did;
- and what they said (interesting quotes).

> Encourage the group to organise themselves so that they can all work on the map at the same time. This might, for example, involve dividing up the journey into four sections with a subgroup working on each of the sections.

> If the group is a large one, then further interesting jobs can be created by adding colour, pictures, or collage pieces to the map. If any illustrative material is too large to fit onto the map, then coloured wool can be used to join the material to the relevant place on the map.

USING THE SKETCH MAP

INFORMAL DISCUSSION: It is quite possible that the process of making the sketch map as a group has already involved a fairly comprehensive informal review of the activity. In terms of the four-stage reviewing sequence (page 13), the map-making task only requires the group to recall the facts (stage one), but it is likely that while making the map, the conversation takes people naturally into later stages of the reviewing sequence ('expressing', 'examining' and 'exploring').

> The reviewer can assist this review process by encouraging informal discussion if it is not happening naturally - by asking questions now and again during the map-making.

> Alternatively, the reviewer can make a mental or written note of review points as they come up, and can summarise these points when the map is completed.

ORGANISED DISCUSSION: If discussion becomes so intense that map-making comes to a standstill, the reviewer can suggest two courses of action: either resolve the issue before continuing, or save it for discussion once the map has been completed.

SEARCHING FOR REVIEW TOPICS: If the journey has been an independent one, or the reviewer was not directly involved, then asking the group to make a sketch map is an excellent way of finding out what happened, and what issues may be worth exploring during a later stage of the review. This can be a time-consuming way of establishing a reviewing agenda, but using a sketch map as a SEARCH TECHNIQUE is likely to result in a much more interesting and worthwhile agenda than simply asking the group what they want to talk about.

REVIEWING THE MAP-MAKING

Map-making is itself an interesting group task which can be worth reviewing, especially if there are interesting comparisons with what happened on the journey. For example:

"If only you had worked together like this during the journey!"

SOUNDTRACK is a visual method of transferring learning from one situation to another.

Young people may find it difficult to believe that an activity such as making an animal out of newspaper has anything to do with helping them to get on better with their parents. They may find it equally difficult to believe that abseiling down a waterfall can help them to get a job. If there are any connections to be made between activity-based learning and situations outside the course, then 'soundtrack' is an effective method for bringing out these potential connections.

EXAMPLE 1: PAPER ANIMAL (LEVEL OF TRANSFER)

The most important feature of 'soundtrack' is that it is designed to find *the most specific level* at which transfer can happen. Using the paper animal as an example, it could be said (at a very *general* level) that the activity increased a young person's confidence with the result that they now have the confidence to talk more openly with their parents. A more *specific* level of transfer would result from (for example) finding out that (a) there were similarities between the group conflict during the activity and the kind of conflict experienced at home, and that (b) the young person played a key part in resolving the conflict during the activity. 'Soundtrack' helps individuals to produce a 'script' summarising their achievement (in this example their achievement in resolving the conflict), and then helps them to identify parallels with another situation in which their successful strategy can be applied.

THE IDEAL STARTING POINT

The ideal starting point for 'soundtrack' is immediately following a significant individual or group achievement. (The 'individual' examples provided can be readily adapted for groups). The experience may have already been partly reviewed. The satisfied participants may already be thinking about repeating the experience in some way. But the chances are that they are thinking about repeating the *activity* rather than about repeating the *experience.*

EXAMPLE 2: TRANSFERRING LEARNING FROM AN EXPEDITION

> Tell or write the outline story of your expedition and divide the story into about six stages. (Alternatively base this on one significant event from the expedition.)

> Make a strip CARTOON (one picture for each stage) with the story *below* each picture and with speech or thought bubbles *above* each picture. The bubbles should capture the essence of what you were saying or thinking at the time.

> Now try to draw a new strip cartoon above the expedition story, using as many of the bubbles as possible, and changing as few words as possible. (The new strip cartoon might be about fundraising, campaigning, organising a club, or setting up a business). A four-part bubble sequence might read:

1) *"We could never do it! How could we get the money and equipment?"*
2) *"We've achieved the impossible already - just getting everything set up and ready to go. Let's hope it all works out."*
3) *"I'd never have made it if it hadn't been for the others - that's what we all said. It was a brilliant team effort."*
4) *"There's not many people who thought we'd go through with it all. They said we didn't have the experience - but now we have!"*

EXAMPLE 3: CLIMBING

> Sketch your climbing route on A4 paper.

> Overlay transparent plastic and add bubbles to show what you were saying and thinking at different points of the climb.

> Add comments from spectators if they affected you in any way.

> Lift off the plastic film, and talk with a partner about other situations (in your own experience) which this pattern of words could fit. If none come to mind, then wipe off some words (starting with those specific to climbing) until you can think of one.

> Describe or sketch the similar situation. See how the words fit and discuss any similarities and differences.

> Choose a future occasion in which there are likely to be challenges or difficulties (the next activity or "back home"), and produce a sketch or strip cartoon (including speech and thought bubbles) to show how you would like things to work out.

SPEAKING as if you are another person is a way both of finding out what it might be like in their shoes, and of showing how well you know them.

Understanding events from different points of view can be partly achieved by observing and listening to others. One test of how well someone has noticed and listened to another is to ask them to act like the other person. If people's acting skills are not highly developed, then it is important to start with exercises which require only a minimal level of acting skill. One such exercise is 'egoing' which is described here as a method for the reviewing of activities. It involves people speaking for others *in the first person* in answer to questions about recent activities.

EGOING

'Egoing' is best used after several activities have been experienced together, and when there is a supportive climate in the group.

> Individuals (or pairs) write down three questions to ask to each other person in the group about the activities. Only one of the three questions should be in any way critical. The questions might be: *Which activity did you least enjoy, and why? How do you rate your performance as a group member? Do you sometimes talk too much?*

> All sit on chairs in a circle (preferably without best friends sitting together). The reviewer chooses someone to sit on the floor in front of the person on their left. *Comfortable* physical contact helps to reduce any sense of isolation felt by the person sitting on the floor: ideally, they lean back against their partner's legs and their partner rests a hand on their shoulder.

> Someone roughly opposite reads out a question which is intended for the person sitting on the floor, naming the person being addressed: e.g. *"Brian, which activity have you enjoyed most?"*

> The person being asked the question (Brian) remains silent and motionless while the person seated above and behind answers, as if they are that person: e.g. *"Finger-painting. I really got involved in that. I wished we'd had longer. I was half-way through my second painting when it was time to stop."*

> Everyone in the group has the chance of asking at least one question. Throughout this period, the person on the floor says nothing. (It is also preferable for them to write nothing.) The questions and answers continue for a fixed time (say 5 minutes) but can be extended or shortened at the reviewer's discretion.

> When time is up, the person on the floor returns to their seat, and is invited (but not forced) to comment on the experience. Rather than (laboriously) going through the 'correct' answers for each question, it is better for the person who has been silent to pick out the answers that were 'spot on' and any that were wildly out. It is also interesting if they give a rough indication of the speaker's overall accuracy (say) expressed as a percentage.

▲ Young people generally find this to be a fascinating process in all roles - as askers, as speakers and when being spoken for. This method extends known concentration spans, but ...

▼ ... if there is not a supportive atmosphere in the group, this method can turn into an underhand way of 'getting at' people - if a string of 'mean' questions are asked. As a precaution against this: clarify relevant ground rules (including the right to pass); start the round with people who are likely to receive 'kind' questions (to set a precedent of sensitivity); and restrict people to the questions which they have written down (if these are likely to be more thoughtful and sensitive than spur of the moment ones).

◆ People being spoken for often express surprise at how well the person acting knows them. Quiet people can be very pleased that someone has put their thoughts into words and spoken up for them.

◆ Should the reviewer join in? The advantages of doing so are:
- speaking for someone else is a useful way of demonstrating the method;
- group members are less likely to opt out if the reviewer has chosen to opt in;
- being spoken for by a group member often reveals misunderstandings of which the reviewer was not previously aware.

TELLING STORIES is the method that young people will naturally use to tell others about their experiences of activity-based learning. There are, of course, many ways in which the reviewer can intervene in this natural process - and there are many good reasons for doing so. How people talk about their experiences indicates what they are learning and how the experience is affecting their development.

> *"New experiences will be more valuable if there are also good opportunities to tell new stories.*
> *Many of our experiences tend to get squeezed into ready-made storylines which don't do justice to the experience. People whose 'stories' have got into the papers know all too well how their own personal experience can get distorted to fit what the newspaper wants to tell its readers. The new world that activities can open up would be lost or trivialised in a similar way if we rush to squeeze new experiences into clichéd storylines.*
> *Stories are more likely to fit new experiences if they are original and home-grown."* [16]

MEMORY GAME

This method demonstrates that no single person has a complete picture of the event. One person sits in the storyteller's chair and starts giving a detailed account of what happened. If any listener thinks the storyteller has omitted any detail, they change places with the storyteller and continue until challenged - and so on.

RE-LIVING THE ACTIVITY

This way of telling the story brings the experience back to life. Each person in turn sits in the storyteller's chair to tell part of the story of a group activity from their own point of view *in the present tense.* (For a group of six people each person tells no more than one-sixth of the whole story.)

SAME AND DIFFERENT

This story-telling method emphasises the individually different experiences within a group activity. Following a group activity, one person tells the story of their experience for about one minute. Listeners note down three points that were similar to their own experience, and three points that were different. The next person tells their story based on the three *different* points which they noted, while listeners record six points as before. Either complete the round, or stop it and ask each remaining person to read out the items on their 'different' lists.

FINDING THE BONES

This summarising method helps to identify the essence of a story. In pairs (after a demonstration), one person gives a one or two minute account of the activity, emphasising their feelings and experiences. The listener then helps the speaker to reduce the story to a few sentences, then to one sentence, then to a phrase (or three words), then to one word. The sentence, phrase and word are recorded by the listener and given to the speaker. In new pairs, and in new roles (speakers are now listeners and vice versa) the exercise is repeated. End with three ROUNDS: single words, then phrases, then sentences.

DRESSING THE SKELETON

This creative reviewing method assists the transfer of learning. As a follow up to 'FINDING THE BONES', each person sums up their story in ten 'feeling' words (or short phrases) and writes them down in the order in which these feelings were experienced. All papers are put into a hat. The reviewer pulls out one paper and records the list on a poster for all to see. The group now brainstorms all the different situations which might fit this skeleton story. The 'owner' of the list is now presented with the poster and the process is repeated for each other list (either in the whole group or in subgroups). If the original story was a positive learning experience, the 'brainstormed' ideas might include situations in which the young person may want to apply what was learned.

Audio TAPE-RECORDERS have many uses as a reviewing aid. This page describes variations of one basic reviewing method using a tape-recorder.

RADIO NEWS

Announce the reviewing task after the activity, providing a written summary of the key points. For example:
> Your reviewing task is to produce a five minute radio programme about the activity.
> Everyone in the group should take part in the recording.
> Most of the recording should be carried out as if it has been made during the activity itself.
> Once the tape-recorder is switched on do not use the pause button: you have five minutes' continuous recording time.
> You have ten minutes' preparation time before switching on the tape-recorder.
> Each person should choose an aspect of the activity they want to be questioned about, and should then write down clearly one or two opening questions to be asked by the reporter.
> Also: choose a reporter (or reporting team); decide on the order of interviews; prepare any sound effects; and decide how to finish.

VARIATIONS

SHORTER BRIEF: The instructions can be simplified: "You have fifteen minutes to produce a five minute radio programme about the activity."

LONGER TERM: The group is given the task of creating a tape in stages over a few different activities.

EARLIER START: Tapes can be recorded before the activity (about expectations and intentions), or during the activity (commentaries by observers or participants), as well as afterwards (as described above).

BIGGER AUDIENCE: The task can be made more real if part of the purpose is to inform others about the experiences. Tapes can be copied and circulated, or can accompany a slide show presentation, or can even be sent to the local radio station. (First check with the radio station about the recording quality necessary.)

TAPE-RECORDING

▲ Tape-recording can highlight significant moments or incidents and encourages reflection about them.

▼ Tape-recording can be an anticlimax if the quality of the recording or playback is poor.

◆ The presence of a tape-recorder changes the levels of participation in a group; it can encourage some group members to speak up more, but may intimidate others. However, quieter people may speak up more than usual if the recording is made in smaller groups or in a series of one-to-one interviews.

ADVANTAGES OVER VIDEO

The advent of video has certainly created new possibilities for reviewing (see the VIDEO section), but sound-only recording still retains many advantages over sound-and-vision technology.

▲ Tape-recording is cheaper, is easier to use and use well. (It is much easier to waste time with video unless its use is carefully planned - and restricted.)

▲ Tape-recording is likely to encourage deeper reflection on what happened as there are no visual distractions.

▲ Tape-recording encourages people to listen to each other, and it encourages people to pay more attention to what they themselves are saying.

◆ Tape-recorders can also be used for recording: PREDICTIONS, ACTION POINTS, OBJECTIVES, OBSERVATIONS, or PRESENTATIONS. Various uses of cam-corders and tape-recorders are described in the PLAYBACK section.

UPS AND DOWNS

UPS AND DOWNS (or highs and lows) can be readily communicated using the active or graphic methods described in this section.

MOVING HANDS UP AND DOWN

One of the most direct ways of finding out young people's 'ups and downs' is to ask them, while sitting in a circle, to move their hands up and down while someone talks through the activity being reviewed. Differences are more likely to show up if participants first record a number for particular moments or stages of the activity:
(e.g. 10 = high = hands up; 0 = low = hands on the floor).
Discussion can be prompted (if necessary) by encouraging young people to look around and ask questions if anyone else's position interests or surprises them.

◆ For a more dramatic (but less comfortable) version substitute 'heads' for 'hands'. On a larger scale (though not in a circle) participants move up and down steps, a sloping embankment, or a hillside!

WALKABOUT: PAIRED CONVERSATIONS

Unlike the examples above, this variation does not emphasise the whole group profile, but is geared more to stimulating paired conversations using a number and a word as a starting point.
> Spread some large sheets of paper on the floor, each with a title describing an incident, event, or stage of an activity to be reviewed. (There should be at least one sheet of paper for every two people.)
> All walk around and, under each title, writes their name, a number (0 = low, 10 = high) and a corresponding feeling under each title.
> All then walk around, find partners and talk for (say) one minute each to their partners about each other's number and feeling.
> After two minutes, this is repeated with a new partner at a new sheet of paper.
> Continue until everyone has spoken to everyone else, or until everyone has visited each paper.

◆ A lot can be reviewed in a short time using this method.

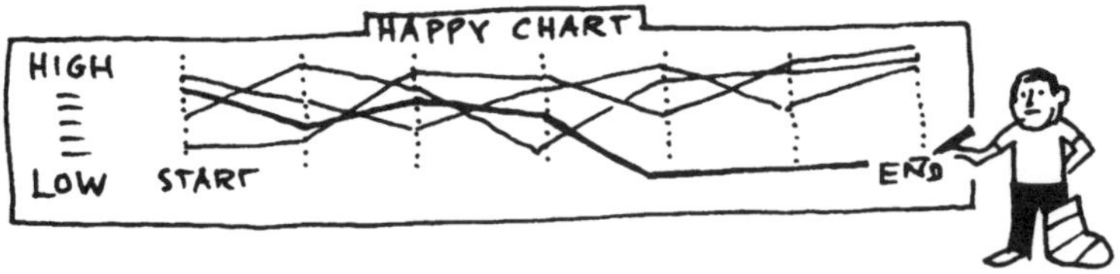

HAPPY CHART

This is a method for recording ups and downs on a graph.

> The event to be 'charted' is divided into about ten parts. (To bring out individual differences, include moments when people seemed to be going through *different* experiences from each other.)

> Each person records a number from minus five to plus five for each of the ten or so occasions that have been agreed. They are now ready either to make an individual chart or to contribute to a giant one ...

> Each person takes a different coloured pen and draws their line on a large chart (approx. 2 metres long), signing their line at each end.

> If there are not enough colours to go round, symbols can be used.

> Now follow up anything interesting that has been said during the making of the chart, as well as asking new questions such as:

What would this chart tell a visitor about the group? How did others affect your ups and downs? How did you affect the ups and downs of others? Would you have liked your own graph line to have a different shape? How could you have 'lifted' yourself or other people?

> Individuals can predict their 'Happy Chart' before an activity and compare this with the chart they make after the activity.

> To encourage awareness of others, ask individuals to guess each other's charts, and then compare guessed charts with real ones.

▲ Each method described on these two pages provides a quick and easy way of prompting individuals to express their feelings; they stimulate interest in how others have been feeling during an activity; and they help participants to feel more noticed and understood by others, but ...

▼ ... individuals can feel ignored and resentful if the pace is so rushed that they do not have a chance to follow up their non-verbal statement with a verbal one.

◆ One of the quicker methods above can be used as a regular review item, but as the 'high-low' dimension produces just one emotional profile of an activity, other opportunities for expressing feelings should also be offered. [17]

VIDEO is rarely used well in reviewing but, with careful planning, video gives access to a useful variety of reviewing methods.

Careful planning and control is necessary to avoid what can easily become an expensive and time-consuming diversion from activity-based learning. Two apparently opposite strategies are recommended in this section: the first (for the video and drama specialist) is to use video work as the central activity of a programme; the second (for non-specialists) is to be highly selective in its use so that it does not take over and dominate a programme.

MAKING TWO VIDEOS

VIDEO 1: A group of young people decide to make a video. It might be for fun, for entertainment, for a local study, for promoting their project, or for campaigning on an issue.

VIDEO 2: This is the 'review' video. This video tells the 'inside story' of how the group made VIDEO 1.

> Organise video skills training sessions and planning sessions for the making of both videos (even though VIDEO 2 might initially be a staff responsibility).

> At the start of each session, clips from VIDEO 2 (the inside story) are shown and reviewed.

▲ VIDEO 2 helps young people to reflect on the processes involved in making VIDEO 1, and brings out issues that will help them to learn to work together more effectively.

▼ It can be difficult getting the balance right: it is up to the reviewer to find the right balance between attention given to the process (VIDEO 2) and attention given to the product (VIDEO 1).

◆ The combination of both kinds of video can produce an interesting result. For example, a video of young people's sketches and raps about 'healthy living' also included some of the behind-the-scenes work involved in making them. [18]

MAKING A REVIEW VIDEO

This method is suitable for beginners. No editing is required, so the film is ready to be played back straight after the activity. It does depend on planning skills and on the discipline of restricting filming to a fixed schedule. Those who are to be responsible for filming (possibly the whole group) are asked to produce a detailed filming schedule to fit into a fixed time limit. A sample schedule is shown below. The name of the camera person should be shown by each job.

SAMPLE FILMING SCHEDULE (for 15 minutes replay time)

1 minute: briefing for the activity	(person A)
1 minute: planning/preparing for the activity	(B)
1 minute: end of planning - announcement of plan	(C)
1 minute: start of activity	(D)
1 minute: 10 minutes later	(E)
1 minute: 10 minutes later	(F)
5 minutes: a half minute interview with each participant during the action (assuming 10 participants)	(A-K)
1 minute: 20 minutes before finishing	(G)
1 minute: 10 minutes before finishing	(I)
1 minute: the last minute of the activity	(J)
1 minute: initial reactions on finishing the activity	(K)

▲ Videos are a useful aid for informing people who were not directly involved - inspiring discussion or follow-up work.

▲ Videos provide useful feedback to people practising specific skills such as interview, presentation or sports skills.
See CARTOONS and PLAYBACK and RADIO NEWS for further uses of video.

▼ Video shows the activity, but it may not show the experience; commentaries or 'voice-overs' should be encouraged during playback if the video does not tell the full story.

▼ Watching an unedited video, and editing a video are both very time-consuming; try working to a strict filming schedule (see above).

▼ Young people may need a second viewing to get over laughs and embarrassment, and to notice other aspects of what is happening.

◆ The 'low tech' version, ACTION REPLAY, (video without a video), has many advantages over the 'high tech' version as a *reviewing* aid.

The sequence of reviewing methods below is useful for reviewing independent activities when the reviewer knows little or nothing about what happened. The sequence can be applied to any journey, expedition, or outing, or to any 'less mobile' project where young people have experienced real responsibility, such as during a service project.

PREPARATION: BEFORE THE ACTIVITY

PLAN: The group makes a plan which includes each person's general responsibilities as a group member, and any special responsibilities.
TAPE-RECORDING: Each person talks for a minute about their responsibilities and about any hopes or concerns they have about the activity.

REVIEW STAGE ONE: EXPERIENCE

SKETCH MAP: After the activity, the group make a large SKETCH MAP, showing significant events such as decisions made, incidents (funny or serious), changes of mood, remembered quotes, observations, etc. (For less mobile activities, use a time-line or CARTOONS.)

REVIEW STAGE TWO: EXPRESS

HAPPY CHART (1): Referring to the map, line or cartoon, divide up the experience into about ten stages and make a group HAPPY CHART.

REVIEW STAGE THREE: EXAMINE

HAPPY CHART (2): While examining the patterns, pay attention to scores at any point where individual responsibility was important.
PLAYBACK: Play back the tape-recording made at the start of the expedition, pausing on request for comments or questions.
FEEDBACK: Check whether each young person has had fair and balanced feedback on their responsibilities. Provide extra opportunities for feedback where necessary.

REVIEW STAGE FOUR: EXPLORE

ACTION POINTS: Discuss what responsibilities individuals would like to take on - whether during another activity or in another setting.

This reviewing sequence helps to increase the levels of support and co-operation in a group, thus providing a sound base from which difficult or sensitive issues can be tackled. The activity should have created situations in which everyone needed to give and receive help.

PREPARATION: BEFORE THE ACTIVITY

A strong emphasis is given to the fact that it is a group activity, and that safety, success and enjoyment will depend on the extent to which people help each other.

REVIEW STAGE ONE: EXPERIENCE

ROUNDS: My personal high point ... my personal low point ... what I found most difficult ... what I found surprisingly easy ...

ACTION REPLAYS (1): Ask the group to re-enact five situations from the activity which demonstrate the different moods of the group.

REVIEW STAGE TWO: EXPRESS

ACTION REPLAYS (2): Discuss issues arising, focusing on examples of co-operation (or lack of it).

SUPPORT SCULPTURES (1): Young people discuss in pairs the ways in which they feel that they each helped or encouraged others, and in which they feel that others helped or encouraged them.

REVIEW STAGE THREE: EXAMINE

SUPPORT SCULPTURES (2): Each person takes it in turn to stand in the middle of the room. They then bring in others closer to them depending on how much 'support' they feel they received from each person in the group. (See HUMAN SCULPTURES for further stages.)

REVIEW STAGE FOUR: EXPLORE

ACTION POINTS: Try to summarise the discussion into a few key points about how young people can maintain and develop group co-operation.

INDEPENDENCE: This sequence is useful preparation for groups to carry out more independent activities in the outdoors or in the local community.

notes and references

Most of the methods described in Chapter Three have been learned and developed 'on the job' - in response to the needs and interests of young people, and as a result of working creatively with inspiring partners and teams. Some of these methods can be traced back to written sources, but there are very few written sources about the reviewing of activities. Wherever original or useful sources are known, they are mentioned below or on page 139.

1 page 24: Tojo Rathour, course participant, quoted in Whitfield W. (1991). *Learning by Achievement*, Youth Work Press.
2 page 24: young unemployed woman, course participant, quoted in Smith M. (1983). *The City Challenge Tutor*, Outward Bound Trust.
3 page 33: Greenaway, R. (1983). Brathay Hall Trust. Unpublished course report of a Trident Trust residential course.
4 page 34-5: All quotations are from Whitfield W. (1991). Working with the Arts, Youth Work Press. The original source for 'ART AS A TOOL' was the Nottingham County Council Leisure Services information pack: *Team Resources for Youth.*
5 page 37: 'Computer Cards' is described in Dearling A., and Armstrong H., (1981). *The Youth Games Book*, I.T. Resource Centre; in Hunt, J. and Hitchin, P. (1986). *Creative Reviewing, Groundwork*; and in Ball, Davill, Eastwood and Holt (1987). *Worth the Risk*, Save the Children Fund.
6 page 39: For the use of cartoons in helping young people to avoid peer group pressure see: Priestley, P. and McGuire, J. (1985). *Offending Behaviour,* Batsford Academic.
7 page 54: Greenaway, R. (1990). *More than Activities* p 18, Save the Children Fund.
8 page 59: also see 'Visual Metaphors' in Jennings, S. (1986). *Creative Drama in Groupwork*, Winslow Press.
9 page 67: 'Advice Endeavour' training course for young people in Clydebank, inspired by Stratchlyde Regional Council's policy document *Partners in Power* (1990).
10 page 69: Liebmann, M. (1986). *Art Therapy for Groups: A Handbook of Themes Games and Exercises*, Croom Helm Ltd and Brookline Books.
11 page 87: The Barrowfield Project, quoted in *More Than Activities* (see note 7).
12 page 89: Teenage Action Project, Blantyre (training by 'Advice Endeavour').
13 page 91: *More Than Activities* p 46 (see note 7).
14 page 94: also see *Art Therapy for Groups* (see note 10 above).
15 page 95: Clydesdale Youth Project (training by 'Advice Endeavour').
16 page 102: *More Than Activities* p 15 (see note 7).
17 page 107: *More Than Activities* p 48 (see note 7).
18 page 108: Healthy Noises Conference (1991). Central Association of Youth Clubs.

4 SETTINGS

Even in the far from ideal surroundings of a prison, it was possible to do something to change the setting so that new styles of learning and new kinds of relationships were possible. It was relatively easy to shift the furniture and change the immediate setting; it was not so easy to influence the organisational setting:

The teacher took a risk. Instead of hovering near the emergency button in her cramped, windowless classroom, she helped the students to shift the desks. Together, they re-arranged the furniture to create some floor space for the activity ... Their review was well under way when the door burst open. "Showers!" called the prison officer. The review came to an abrupt end. [1]

What is possible in any review setting is influenced to varying degrees by the values of the organisation and by the nature of the programme, or course, club, project, scheme, curriculum etc.. This chapter provides examples of different reviewing strategies being applied across a number of programme settings: school, youth work, youth social work, youth training, work experience, employee development, residential care, and finally The Duke of Edinburgh's Award which spans all the above settings. Whatever the setting (whether listed here or not), it should be clear from the examples provided that reviewing can play a vital role in the personal and social development of all young people - wherever they are.

informal discussion

These disaffected young people needed little persuasion to review an activity which was fun and in which they all achieved success:

The next day we went horse-riding. A motley crew of hats,

duffle coats, cagoules and Wellington boots, cantering wildly over Welsh hills for two hours... Even Jim and Dirk, who were adamant that there was 'no way' they'd consider clambering on a horse, took courage and joined the carnival. Nine Bristol kids trotted out of the yard as a scenario for a Thelwell cartoon, and two hours later cantered in as John Wayne leading his cavalry troop. The ride dominated the talk for the rest of the day.

'Did you see me ...'

'How about when ...'

'What a laugh as Lester ...'

That evening at midnight, after vegetable stew and a night hike, they were still re-living the high moments. [2]

learning from each other

One simple technique can change learning habits:

After each bit of the project, we got together with the design teacher to talk about the work. We had a checklist so we could fill in what progress we'd made and what we'd learned to do. At first it was mainly the teacher talking to us, but after a bit we started talking to each other more. In the end we were learning more from each other than from the teacher! [3]

sequenced discussion

A sequenced discussion can make an interesting activity even more interesting, revealing more surprises and bringing out more learning:

We looked at rock climbing in different ways. First there was how I did it and how I felt - not too good as it happens. Everyone went through that. Then we all discussed how we thought each other had done, which surprised me, as quite a few thought I'd done okay. Finally we got round to thinking about how we had all helped each other as a group, and how it was easier to take help from some people than from others. [4]

regularly reviewing objectives

Reviewing was an integral part of this activity-based course. Course objectives and individual objectives were regularly reviewed:

Based upon a philosophy of learning through action, fun and reviewing, the course was a 50/50 mix of indoor and outdoor activities. Each activity was carefully selected and designed to be a challenging and exciting vehicle for bringing about learning in accordance both with the course aims and the objectives which the participants set themselves. To this end the setting of individuals' objectives at the start of the course, and the constant reviewing of activities in relation to these objectives, was in reality the most important aspect ...

The final day saw the young people setting new personal objectives for their return to work, and it was here that the learning from the course began to have direct relevance for the workplace and for the organisation as a whole. [5]

developing learning skills

These DO's and DON'Ts for developing learning skills are designed to encourage 'instructors' to give 'participants' more opportunities for learning from what they do.

DO show that all participants have a contribution to make BY making sure that you take notice of their views.

DO encourage participants to identify and correct their own mistakes BY providing models and guiding them with questions.

DO allow them time to work something out for themselves BY giving them pondering time.

DO develop the participants' interest in learning to do things for themselves BY discussing with them how they intend to go about learning something.

DON'T belittle participants' attempts at learning BY laughing at them or comparing them unkindly with others.

DON'T give unrealistic feedback BY giving undue praise or over critical comment. [6]

reviewing work experience (HOW NOT TO DO IT)

This description of how not to set up and review work experience can be readily turned into constructive ideas for doing it well:

Work experience often lacks educational value for two reasons. First, without systematic reflection it becomes a vicarious experience from which few lessons are learnt ...

Too often the young person, having completed some work experience, is slotted back into a timetable where there is no room either for the reflective learning needed or for identifying the new experience. Or again, the very considerable experience gained by many young people from part-time work receives no acknowledgement in schools.

A second and connected reason for work experience being non-educational is the non-developmental nature of it. Too often it is planned without reference to the previous experience the pupil has had or to what subsequently he or she may be doing. [7]

"coming out of my shell"

This unemployed young man voluntarily attended a local activity group and greatly valued his experiences of reviewing:

I've known these boys since we were at primary school, and you thought you knew them, but we're really only just getting to know each other. All of a sudden there's this new bit of them that you've never seen before. It really amazed me. It was a great experience. I've never actually realized before the potential we had. The only thing you ever came in for before was a game of pool: now you find out all sorts of things you never knew.

I don't know how to explain it, but it seemed to be that, while we were having these discussions, everybody was getting into things you don't usually get into, getting to know each other. The discussions we were having: they were meaning something. You had to read out your own personal feelings, and I had to do it first. It wasn't as hard as I thought it would be. That was the turning point for me: when I'd seen that I could open up in front of these other guys. It was a great experience.

If that group was still there, the other boys might not be in jail, because they were getting all sorts of kicks out of it. I found that I came out of my shell even more, and could speak about things that I wouldn't normally speak about. I think that's what that group done for me. It just brought me right out, made me more aware of things that's happening. Through that group I broke away from the street life that I was used to: cutting several links - not all links - I've still got my pals. [8]

transforming meetings

In this children's home, giving young people more responsibility for meetings was the key to success:

We were having residents' meetings every week, and they were turning into what the staff called 'greetin' meetings'. All it was was the young people coming to the meetings with a catalogue of complaints - and it was a bad experience not only for the young people, but for the staff as well. So we decided not to have a residents' meeting every week. We would just have one whenever the young people wanted it. We said "We'll leave it up to you to decide when you want meetings".

We didn't have any residents' meetings for several weeks and then one day, one of the youngsters came to staff and said "We'd like to have a meeting this evening." We sat down and had a meeting and it was a really good experience for everybody. The young people had set up their own agenda. From then on we got back to having a regular residents' meeting and it worked really well. O.K. we had one or two that weren't happy with them, but it wasn't compulsory, and the kids felt it wasn't forced upon them. We had put the onus back on them and said "We're not having these meetings because it suits us - we're having them because it's what you want". From then on it became a regular occurrence. [9]

reviewing in THE DUKE OF EDINBURGH'S AWARD

This draft document about 'The Award in Schools' emphasises the value of reviewing:

Reviewing should be a natural part of all activities. Its purpose is to:
- ensure the relevance of the activity and intended learning to the young people concerned, drawing on feelings and relationships to encourage the group members to be aware of their interdependency;
- change goals, if necessary, by agreement, as a result of experience;

- deepen self-awareness, develop empathy with and concern for others in the group, taking account of everyone's view and feelings;
- emphasise the purpose of the activity, its importance to each individual, and thus enhance learning;
- establish an acceptance that reviewing is a natural part of all activities, necessary if full value is to be obtained.

Much of this can be carried out by an experienced teacher on the hoof, as the activity proceeds, but time also needs to be set aside to emphasise the importance of reviewing. Unless adequate reflection on what is happening and being experienced takes place, there is a danger that obsessive concern for completing the task can take over at the expense of personal learning.

Reviews are particularly important if things do not work out as planned. What at first sight may seem to be failure can usually, with skilful leadership, be used to draw out positive learning. The intention should always be to complete the task having learnt as much as possible from participative reviewing and with good feelings about the future. [10]

---

notes and references

1 From an interview by the author.
2 White R. (1980) *Absent with Cause.* Routledge and Kegan Paul.
3 Hunt, J. and Hitchin, P. (1986). *Creative Reviewing,* Groundwork, 3 Meathop Fell, Meathop, Cumbria LA11 6QZ.
4 MSC, (1985). *Residential Training in YTS: Youth Training Scheme Manual,* Manpower Services Commission, Sheffield.
5 Barnett, T. (Bradford City Council) (Feb. 1986). *Training for Transition, No.2* Local Government Training Board.
6 MSC (1983). *Learning: Youth Training Scheme: Practitioner's Guide 2,* adapted from work by Sylvia Downs, Pat Perry, and Helen Ryan of the Occupational Research Unit at UWIST, Cardiff.
7 Pring, R. (1984). *Personal and Social Education in the Curriculum,* Hodder and Stoughton.
8 From an interview by the author in *Adventures in Youth Social Work* (1988), Ideas Exchange, Scottish I.T. Resource Centre.
9 From an interview by the author in *What Works Well for Young People in Care?* (1992), Endeavour Scotland.
10 Huskins, J. (1992). *Learning for Life: The Award and Schools, A Guide for Teachers: A draft document for consultation,* The Duke of Edinburgh's Award.

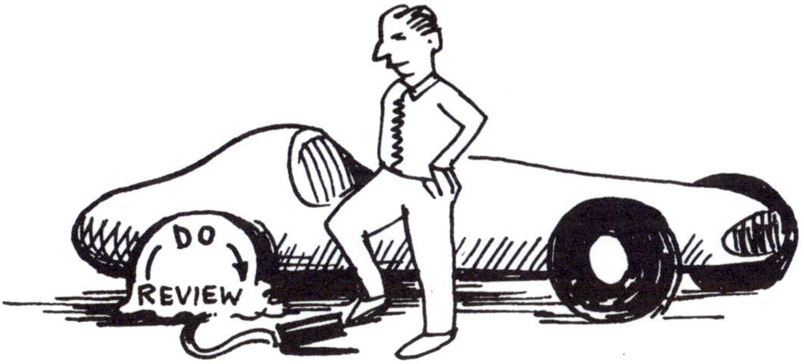

5 ISSUES

This chapter outlines some of the issues which can prevent reviews from getting started. Given the many reasons why activities *should* be reviewed, why can excuses be so easy to come by? There seem to be two main types of resistance. Some people are resistant to reviewing because, despite liking the idea, they are not sure how best to go about it. Others are resistant because they still need to be convinced that reviewing is worth doing.

The process of developing reviewing skills does often require an attitude shift of some kind in order to support new ways of working. The kinds of 'shift' that might be needed are:

- towards a more 'adult' way of working;
- towards a different kind of 'culture': whether making an informal setting more purposeful and structured, or whether making a formal setting more open and flexible;
- towards a more person-centred approach: taking individual experiences and wishes more into account;
- towards a more non-directive approach: involving young people more in decision-making both within and about the programme;
- towards a more holistic approach: using a wider range of methods borrowed from other disciplines or subject areas.

In each issue about reviewing which is listed below, readers might recognise the situation, even if their own particular setting is different. Each issue is followed by a response which should help reviewers to unblock any resistance, whether it is in their own minds, or in the minds of young people or other staff. [Refer to 'groupwork' in the main index, for consideration of issues which are more to do with groupwork than with the reviewing of activities.]

wrong experience, wrong message

"Is reviewing really necessary?"

Without reviewing, many potential benefits are lost (see for example pp 20-23). But more significantly, without reviewing, many supposedly 'developmental' activities can be counterproductive. This is illustrated by the example of a young woman, Susan, who took part in an outdoor personal development course. She was asked to navigate on a mountain walk, but she made a route-finding mistake. From that point on, Susan felt less inclined to volunteer or take risks. None of this was reviewed because it was not part of the course culture to do so. A course which was designed to build confidence and encourage people to take risks was having precisely the opposite effect. Without a review, the leader was unable to learn much about the negative consequences of this event. Without a review, Susan had little chance to gain anything positive from the experience. [1]

What we learn, and whether that learning has a positive or negative orientation, depends very much on how we review what we do - or on what we do with experience: "Experience is not what happens to a man; it is what a man does with what happens to him." [2]

expectations

"They're only here for the activities: that's all they were told about. We can't suddenly introduce reviewing."

Next time, ensure that reviewing is an integral part of what young people are offered at the start! Also, agree a purpose so that there is at least one item on the reviewing agenda. *This time*, it may still not be too late to sell the idea of reviewing:

- Point out occasions where participants have already been reviewing without realising it, and offer to build on their natural interest!

- Use MID-ACTIVITY REVIEWING or multi-stage activities in which what is learned from one stage is applied in the next stage.

- If young people's expectations of 'activities' include creative and expressive arts, try using these activities as a means of reviewing previous ones.

motivation

"They say they don't like reviewing, and they don't see the point."

Respond to *both* of these objections: even if only one is stated, the other one will probably also exist.

- Find out what each person likes and dislikes about reviewing, and try to work out alternative ways of reviewing activities in which everyone will participate more readily.

- Point out that asking "What's the point of reviewing?" suggests that they like to have a clear purpose for what they do. Ask them to 'brainstorm' a list of purposes for the activities they are doing, and point out how reviewing can help them to achieve some of those purposes. If the 'brainstorm' only produces words like 'fun', 'enjoyment', 'to have a good time', refer to BEYOND ENJOYMENT (p 43).

equal opportunities

"They can't take part in reviewing ... they haven't got a long enough concentration span / they are disabled / they can't speak English."

Yes they can take part! Everyone can learn from experience. If 'reviewing' simply means 'group discussion', these concerns might apply, but group discussion can be one of the most difficult and demanding ways of reviewing, even for highly articulate people. The answer is to find a suitable method, not to abandon reviewing. A reviewer prepared to make use of a wide range of styles and methods has a much better chance of finding ways in which young people can communicate about their experiences, whatever their ability or 'disability'.

Many of the review techniques described in Chapter 3 have been specifically developed in order to include young people of all abilities in reviewing sessions. [3] Suitable reviewing methods capture young people's interest, enable them to reflect and communicate, and extend their assumed 'concentration spans'. The higher the ability (and flexibility) of the reviewer, the more will concentration problems disappear!

timing

"Things are going really well. Let's not spoil it by stopping for a review just now." Later: "Things aren't going too well. Let's wait until they're a bit happier before we stop for review." Later still: "We've run out of time to do a proper review. Let's start with a review next time." Next time ... the attendance is different, or there are new priorities, or the experience has 'gone cold' and no-one's interested in going over what happened last time. [4]

Reviewers do need to be flexible and to have a good sense of timing, but if the time never seems right, then perhaps it is time for the frustrated reviewer to break down the cycle of excuses and write down a list of the favourable conditions which they are waiting for - and then to make them happen.

risk

"Is there not a danger that reviewing will ..."
"I'm not properly trained in ..."

Development involves risk, and trying anything new is a risk, both for young people and for the reviewer. But reviewing has a 'shallow end' and a 'deep end'. [5] The choice of depth depends on factors such as: the purpose, the reviewer's skill and confidence, and the level at which participants will most readily respond. The BASIC TOOLKIT of eight methods (p 25) provides a relatively low risk start to reviewing. One of the eight methods, ROUNDS (p 90), is particularly useful for finding the right level, and for monitoring reactions to other reviewing methods.

There is also an opposite danger, which arises from not reviewing activities in which strong emotions (whether highs or lows) have been stirred up - and then neglected. Denying young people the opportunity of reviewing in a supportive atmosphere is letting them down, especially if it allows negative feelings or negative messages to 'sink in'.

image

"They'll think it's childish."

For many teenagers, the dividing line between what is seen by them as 'childish' and what is seen by them as 'adult' can be very narrow. This is also the age at which activity-based learning can be particularly valuable and empowering. Respect young people's sensitivities. Tell them: "If there are particular things you don't want to do, just say so, the point of this course is to make you feel good about yourself, not for you to feel ashamed or embarrassed. So you can opt out of anything. You are also welcome to suggest alternative ways of reviewing any activity."

Cajoling, threatening, tricking, rewarding or bribing might result in the young person joining in - but at what cost? (especially if you have previously agreed a ground rule which allows passing). Patience is a more effective and longer-lasting strategy: "The only way to get everyone to participate is to allow everyone not to participate". [6]

informality

"What's wrong with just having a chat?"

Nothing is wrong with just having a chat. But there is likely to be a limit to what can be achieved through reviewing if only informal methods are used. I once worked on a 5 day residential course in which the young people were so keen on chatting, and seemed to be so good at 'reviewing-by-chatting' and at dealing with issues in this informal way, that I simply joined in with their chats and chose not to introduce any structured techniques for reviewing. The individuals in this group got on with each other particularly well, and they just wouldn't stop talking about the course and what it was doing for them! Their conversations were more or less following the learning cycle without any facilitation from me, and everyone was taking part. In my experience, this was a notable exception: unfacilitated chats are rarely of such a high quality.

right experience, wrong message

"Surely it is better spending time getting the experience right? If the experience isn't worthwhile then nothing else will be."

A young participant on a development training course did not believe the positive things that others in the group were saying about him. He was so used to being put down by others, and his self-esteem was so low, that he thought they were being sarcastic. It took two further review sessions for him to accept that they were telling the truth. He had been blocking out the positive messages from the activities. It was in the review sessions that he eventually succeeded in overcoming this personal barrier. For this young person, it was the reviewing which provided the biggest challenge and the most significant learning. [7]

---

notes and references

1 From an interview by the author in *Doing Reviewing* (1992). *Journal of Adventure Education and Outdoor Leadership*, 9(1).
2 Aldous Huxley in *Texts and Pretexts*, (1932). (The preceding example shows that this applies equally to 'woman'!)
3 The successful use of reviewing methods with groups from special schools by Brathay staff, particularly Annie Cooper, resulted in new teaching methods being adopted in the schools involved.
4 Greenaway, R. (1990). *More Than Activities*, Save the Children Fund.
5 Both Donna Brandes (Gamesters' Handbooks) and Jill Baldwin (Active Tutorial Work) encourage workers to value what I have referred to as "working at the shallow end", while Donna Brandes also points out that "people can be quite easily trained to expand upon [the games] and upon their uses".
6 Brandes, D. (1982). *Gamesters' Handbook Two*, Hutchinson.
7 First reported by the author in *Doing Reviewing* (1992). *Journal of Adventure Education and Outdoor Leadership*, 9(1).

6 SKILLS

facilitation: making learning easy

The reviewer's task is to facilitate learning. This means *making learning easy*. Some facilitators of learning seem to get so caught up in complexities, that they lose sight of the fact that their fundamental task is to make things easy. Why bang your head against a brick wall when there's a gate round the corner? This chapter is about the gates round the corner - making learning easy.

Why do some people find it difficult to learn from experience? The previous chapter ended with one explanation - that low self-esteem can be a barrier to learning. The next section, on page 127, describes a method for identifying other barriers to learning (which makes further use of the four stage reviewing sequence introduced in Chapter 1). But there is one significant barrier which this method does not reveal. That is simply the fact that young people are not used to this way of learning.

Once young people realise that they are expected to learn from what they do, rather than learning from being taught, it makes a lot of sense to them. But they may be slow to realise that this is all that is involved. They may not have experienced this way of learning in school. This may be their first encounter with a 'facilitator' who makes learning easy for them! If young people experience 'culture shock' when moving from one learning culture to another, it will take them time to adjust.

You can help young people to 'adapt' by giving clear, simple explanations of the learning process. Make your expectations of them clear, and involve young people as soon as possible in experiencing this new way of learning. A useful introduction is a 10 minute problem-solving activity followed by a 10 minute review. Some young people might 'click' straight away. Others will take longer to adapt to what might well be a brand new learning culture for them. If you introduce young people to activity-based learning by dropping them in it with little explanation, facilitating learning will not be easy!

If your situation allows, a simple way of reinforcing the fact that the learning process is new and different, is to find a location that is new and different (and preferably also comfortable and inspiring). If you have a choice between working in an oppressive environment which brings out the worst in people, or travelling to a wonderful environment in which everyone suddenly starts being friendly towards each other and more grown up, it's well worth making the journey! Once young people are accustomed to activity-based learning, the choice of environment is less critical. And once young people's learning abilities have been 'woken up' in a favourable setting, it should then be easier to review in less ideal environments.

Another way of making learning from experience easy is to say that it is - and then show that it is. Ask the group to come up with a list of all the things that they have learned to do without being taught. These are all examples of learning from experience. Ask which skills were easiest to learn and why. You can follow this up by asking young people to learn a few more skills without being taught. You can then review these activities by asking them how they learned these skills, and what hindered and helped their learning. This will allow them to discover experiential learning theory for themselves! They will also be demonstrating the talents they already have for learning from experience.

assessing young people's reviewing skills

Simply by taking part in reviewing, most young people will be getting better at it. They will be getting more observant. They will be improving their communication skills. They will be more open to learning and more able to learn. But some groups and individuals may not be getting any better at reviewing. How can you find out why some people are not benefitting as much as others? The easiest way to find out is to ask them. But they may not know why. Another way of finding out is to use the four stage reviewing sequence as a 'diagnostic tool'. This involves assessing young people's skills in each of the four stages. The reviewer can think about this on their own, or they can ask the group to assess their own strengths and weaknesses in each of the four stages - both as a group and individually. The example below is for individuals. By changing 'I' and 'me' to 'we' and 'us' it can also be used at a group level.

> THE ACTIVITY: On a scale of 1 (low) to 10 (high), how involved do you get in the activities? What's stopping you from getting more involved? Complete the sentence: "I would put in more effort if ..."

1) EXPERIENCE: On a scale of 1 to 10, how observant do you think you are? What kinds of things do you most notice and think about during activities? Complete the sentence: "I would be more observant if ..."
2) EXPRESS: On a scale of 1 to 10, how much do you express your feelings / say what's on your mind / get your point of view across? Complete the sentence: "It would be easier for me to speak up if ..."
3) EXAMINE: On a scale of 1 to 10, how well do you listen to others? How much do you take part in discussions, and making decisions? Complete the sentence: "I would get more from discussions if I ..."
4) EXPLORE: On a scale of 1 to 10, how willing are you to try out new ways of doing things? How ambitious are you when you set targets? Complete the sentence: "I would be more adventurous if ..."

Now decide which of the four stages needs most 'remedial' attention and search for suitable reviewing methods for that stage, (such as by using the index on page 29). Then experiment in your next review!

using intuition as a reviewer

The above use of the four stage reviewing model can help reviewers to identify the main barriers or 'blocks' to learning. But learning cycles provide only one perspective on reviewing. In amongst the dynamics of activity-based learning, there are many other currents ebbing, flowing and swirling which affect learning and development. Models can help reviewers (and learners) to think more clearly about reviewing, but the reality is that many judgments about reviewing are intuitive ones. These are some of the areas in which intuition is necessary.

CONTRAST VS. CONTINUITY: Sometimes it feels right to use reviewing methods which provide a contrast to what has just been experienced: by following a chaotic activity with a structured review; or by following a structured activity with a free-flowing review; or by following a team activity with time for individuals to reflect. At other times it feels right to stay with the mood of the moment, such as by keeping the energy of the activity flowing with a busy, active review.

SUPPORT AND RISK: Activities which have been challenging may need to be followed by reviews which are comforting. Young people who feel thoroughly 'at home' in an activity may benefit more from a review which provokes and challenges. The reviewer needs to judge when to increase support and when to increase the risk - in a way that results in learning and development.

ACCENTUATE THE POSITIVE VS. ELIMINATE THE NEGATIVE: How much review time do you spend looking at problems, needs, issues, fears, failures, weaknesses, etc.? How much review time do you spend looking at strengths, interests, hopes, skills, achievements, potential, opportunities etc.? If you slice young people in half and work with just one side of them (whether their positive side or their negative side), not very much learning or development is likely to happen. Reviewers should be able to sense and choose the appropriate balance.

learning from experience (as a reviewer)

One way of developing skills as a facilitator of reviews is to apply the four stage reviewing sequence to your own practice. This is how it can be applied.

1) EXPERIENCE (FACTS): Decide how you are going to make a record of your reviewing session. Here are some possibilities.
- TAPE-RECORDER OR VIDEO: With the group's permission, record a review session (or parts of it). This can be dual purpose: the group may also be interested in hearing or seeing themselves on tape.
- OBSERVER: Ask someone (a co-worker?) to make notes during your reviewing session. Ask them if there are particular points you want them to look for. They should record the times of their observations.
- PERSONAL LOG: If there are opportunities during a reviewing session when you are not directly involved, record notes and times yourself, and complete your log soon after the review. Add a list of your 'highs' and 'lows', or make a personal HAPPY CHART.
- FEEDBACK: At the end of a reviewing session, ask some questions to the group, first in ROUNDS, then in general discussion.
A useful series of questions for feedback is: "What was 'just right', 'too much', 'too little'? Why?" followed by "It would have been better if ...")
If you want individual responses, then give out brief questionnaires about the review session before any group discussion about it. Graphs showing individual involvement levels during the session can also result in useful feedback and discussion.

2) EXPRESS (FEELINGS): Either with an interested friend or a supportive colleague, talk through what happened in the session, and your initial reactions to any feedback you have received.

3) EXAMINE (FINDINGS): Try to understand more about why things happened as they did. What does this say about my reviewing? What are my strengths and weaknesses? How could I improve?

4) EXPLORE (FUTURE): In future ... It would be interesting to try ... It would be interesting to find out if ... Next time I will ...

unblocking learning

Young people will be more involved in reviewing if their needs are being met (p 20), and if they are helped to overcome blocks to learning (p 127). The reviewer may intuitively sense these 'needs' and 'blocks' or may have a method of identifying them. Simply talking with young people about "what seems to be getting in the way of learning" will often produce an explanation, and even a solution. A combination of all three strategies (intuition, analysis and discussion) can help the reviewer to get individuals or groups 'unstuck'.

This investigation of needs and blocks will sometimes make things worse before they get better. It may not be possible to satisfy the needs, or overcome the blocks immediately. But through investigation, "what is getting in the way" is likely to become clearer, and the reviewer will be better able to judge the best course of action to take. Options might include:

- turning the 'problem' into the main purpose, and giving it maximum attention;
- putting the 'problem' on one side and proceeding with the review;
- postponing the review while the reviewer takes appropriate action outside the review setting to alleviate the 'problem'.

Another important consideration is that you, the reviewer, may be the block. However well intentioned are your attempts to assist the process of learning, you could be trying too hard.

> *"Leaders who push think they are facilitating process, when in fact they are blocking process ... They think their constant interventions are a measure of their ability, when in fact such interventions are crude and inappropriate ... The wise leader uses the least force required to act effectively."*
> (from 'the Paradox of Pushing' in John Heider's *The Tao of Leadership*).

Consider the possibility that you do not lack skill but that you are trying to use too much.

7 RESOURCES

I learned to review:
- FROM OTHER PEOPLE: by observation, co-working, and word of mouth;
- BY DEVELOPING NEW METHODS: from the need to do so after discovering the limitations of group discussion as a reviewing technique;
- BY ASKING FOR FEEDBACK: from co-reviewers and from young people (if they needed prompting!)
- BY ADAPTING IDEAS from other subject areas.

As I knew of no handbook of reviewing techniques, I had little choice but to use the above strategies. It also happened to be an enjoyable way of learning!

'Learning from others', 'learning from experience', and 'learning from books' are three ways of developing reviewing skills. This chapter allows readers to explore the third option and to find the balance which suits them best.

Depending on how you look at it, there are either very few books about reviewing methods or there is an unending list. My short list of practical books about reviewing includes: *Creative Reviewing*, *Processing the Experience* and *Effective Debriefing*. This variety of terms ('reviewing', 'processing', and 'debriefing', not to mention 'reflection') illustrates a major problem in cataloguing this area of work: - reviewers (whether 'counsellors', 'facilitators', 'instructors', 'assessors', 'leaders', 'teachers', 'therapists', 'trainers', 'tutors', 'social workers', or 'youth workers') do not all talk the same language about reviewing!

This 'language problem' can be turned to advantage by enterprising reviewers prepared to stray a little from their 'home' field - given the interdisciplinary nature of reviewing, and the possibility of adapting ideas from other fields. Therefore a variety of subjects are represented by the books listed on the following pages, including: adventure education, art therapy, developmental counselling, drama therapy, education, developmental groupwork, management development, personal and social education, youth work, youth social work, and youth training.

If readers accept that they don't need to be an art therapist to ask someone to draw a picture, then it is only one small step to refer to *Art Therapy for Groups* and discover many more ideas (simple or advanced) which can be used for reviewing. Similarly, readers don't need to be trained in yoga to ask someone to lie down and think; they don't need a psychology degree to organise a game for young people; or need a training qualification to set up a problem-solving task.

In order to help readers find inspiration in related fields of work, I started by selecting books which are readable by non-specialists, practical, obtainable, and affordable. Unfortunately, there are very few books about reviewing which meet these criteria! But those books which come closest to meeting these needs should readily be found in the lists which follow. In such an interdisciplinary subject there are bound to be large gaps in any reading list. I have attempted to indicate the main subject areas where inspiration for reviewing (and more detailed reading lists) are most likely to be found.

GROUPWORK

Experience and understanding of working with groups provides a useful foundation for trying out new reviewing ideas. The first two titles listed are useful jargon-free introductions to groupwork (but are not specifically about work with young people).

Kindred, M. (1987, Revised Edition). **Once Upon a Group: a book to help members of groups**, (78 pages, £4.50 in 1993), Michael Kindred, 20 Dover Street, Southwell, Notts. NG25 OEZ. This is a practical and readable introduction to groupwork (with useful matchstick figure illustrations).

Houston, G. (1984). **The Red Book of Groups: a systematic approach**, (123 pages, £4.95 in 1993), The Rochester Foundation, 8 Rochester Terrace, London NW1. This is another practical, readable and affordable introduction to groupwork with useful matchstick figure illustrations! It also demonstrates Gestalt concepts in action - a whole-person approach to development.

Button, L. (1974). **Developmental Groupwork with Adolescents**, (206 pages), Unibooks, Hodder and Stoughton, London. Unlike many introductions to groupwork this one is specific to work with *young people* and takes a *developmental perspective* rather than a problem-based one. It is written for teachers and youth workers.

Brown, A. (1979). **Groupwork**, Heinemann, London.

Douglas T. (1978). **Basic Groupwork**, Tavistock Publications.

Heider, J. (1985). **The Tao of Leadership**, Wildwood House Ltd., Hampshire.

Hodge, J. (1985). **Planning for Co-leadership: a practical guide for groupworkers**, Groupvine.

Preston-Shoot, M. (1987). **Effective Groupwork**, (Practical Social Work), Macmillan, London.

REVIEWING

Hunt, J. and Hitchin, P. (1986). **Creative Reviewing**, (60 pages, £6.50 in 1992) Groundwork, 3 Meathop Fell, Meathop, Cumbria LA11 6QZ. Prabhu Guptara's review in the *Training and Development Journal* (Oct 1990) stated that not only was *Creative Reviewing* "unbeatable value", but that it was "the *only* publication available on the essential subject of debriefing after all games, role play, simulations and other exercises." The methods described include action replay, discussion, drawings, learning transfer chart, photographs, poems, review matrix, role play, questionnaire, and storytelling.

Nadler, R. S. and Luckner, J. L. (1990). **Processing the Experience: Theory and Practice**. (158 pages, $22 in 1991) Northern Illinois University, Dekalb, IL 60115. This book draws together ideas from a number of articles published in *The Journal of Experiential Education.* The methods described include: large group discussion, journal writing, dyads, small group discussion, written activity sheets, isolation, drawing.

Williams, T. (1991). **Effective Debriefing: the key to learning**, (64 pages, £28.95 in 1993), British Association for Commercial and Industrial Education, 16, Park Crescent, London W1N 4AP. *Effective Debriefing* provides notes on effective debriefing (i.e. reviewing), guidance on giving and receiving feedback, activities to use when debriefing and guidance on questions to ask.

RECORDING

Both the National Youth Agency and The Open University have produced books about recording experience. NYA titles include: **Starting from Strengths**, **Show What You Know** and **Making the Past Count** (1984). OU titles include: **Building Portfolios** (1988) and **Making Your Experience Count** (1993). The exercises in these books need adapting for use with young people.

Ashforth, D. (1990). **Records of Achievement in the Marketplace**, NFER - Nelson.

Stansbury, D. '**The record of personal experience**' in Burgess, T. and Adams, E. (Eds). (1980) **Outcomes of Education**, Macmillan, London.

Yorkshire and Humberside Regional Examination Board (1987). **Records of Achievement: Recording Residential Experience**, Northern Partnership for Records of Achievement.

GAMES AND EXERCISES

Most of these books focus on the *experience* in experiential learning, generally giving less attention to ways in which experiences can be reviewed, other than through discussion. All of the books listed in this section describe activities with 'built-in' messages and objectives. These activities can be valuable to the reviewer in a number of ways:
- some help to generate and sustain a climate for learning;
- some develop learning skills (e.g. observing, listening, expressing);
- some bring out issues for reviewing (e.g. trust, values, relationships);
- some can be used as reviewing methods.

Brandes, D. and Philips H. (1979). **Gamester's Handbook: 140 Games for Teachers and Group Leaders**; and Brandes, D. (1984). **Gamester's Handbook 2**, Hutchinson, London.

Dearling A., and Armstrong H. (1983, 2nd Edition). **The Youth Games Book**, ITRC, Cordee, 3a De Montfort Street, Leicester, LE1 7HD.

Fleugleman, A. (ed.). (1978). **The New Games Book**; (1981). **More New Games and Playful Ideas**, New Games Foundation, Doubleday, New York.

Forbes-Greene, S. (1983). **The Encyclopaedia of Icebreakers**, Applied Skills Press.

Jennings, S. (1986). **Creative Drama in Groupwork**, Winslow Press, Winslow, Buckinghamshire.

Kirk, R. (1987). **Learning in Action: activities for personal and group development**, Basil Blackwell, Oxford.

Liebmann, M. (1986). **Art Therapy for Groups: A Handbook of Themes Games and Exercises**, Croom Helm Ltd and Brookline Books.

Orlick, T. (1978). **The Cooperative Sports and Games Book: Challenge Without Competition**, Writers and Readers Publishing Co-operative.

Remocker, J. and Storch E. (1979). **Action Speaks Louder: Handbook of Non-verbal Group Techniques**, Churchill Livingstone, Edinburgh; (1982) New York.

PROGRAMMES

These books give more attention to how activities can fit into the framework of a course, programme or curriculum.

Baldwin, J. and Wells, H. (Eds). (1979, 1980, 1981). **Active Tutorial Work**, Books 1-5, Basil Blackwell, Oxford.

Ball, Davill, Eastwood and Holt (1987). **Worth the Risk: creative groupwork with young offenders**, Save the Children Fund, UK.

Department of Education and Science (1989). **Personal and Social Education from 5 to 16**, Curriculum Matters Series No 14, H.M.S.O.

Fine, N. and Macbeth F. (1992). **Playing with Fire: Training for the Creative Use of Conflict**. Youth Work Press.

Greenaway, R. (1990). **More Than Activities**, Save the Children Fund.

Hopson B. and Scally M. (1980, 1981). **Lifeskills Teaching**, Lifeskills Associates, McGraw Hill, Maidenhead.

Kirk, R. and Dennison, Bill (1990). **Do, Review, Learn, Apply: a simple guide to experiential learning**, Blackwell Education, Oxford.

McGuire, J. and Priestley, P. (1985). **Offending Behaviour: Skills and Stratagems for Going Straight**, Batsford Academic and Educational.

Pfeiffer, J.W. and Jones, J.E. (1975). **Handbook of Structured Experiences for Human Relations Training**, 1-5, University Associates, La Jolla, California.

Pickles, T. (1987). **Working with Young People in Trouble: a practical manual**, Scottish Intermediate Treatment Resource Centre, Glasgow.

Priestley, P., McGuire, J. et al (1978). **Social Skills and Personal Problem Solving: A Handbook of Methods**, Tavistock Publications Ltd.

Pring, R. (1984). **Personal and Social Education in the Curriculum**, Hodder and Stoughton.

Schoel, Prouty, and Radcliffe (1988). **Islands of Healing: A Guide to Adventure Based Counseling**, Project Adventure, Inc, Hamilton, MA.

Spragg, D. (1981). **Learning in Action: a framework for social education in the youth opportunities programme**, National Youth Bureau.

EXPERIENTIAL LEARNING

Publications about experiential learning which do not readily fit the headings of previous pages.

Bacon, S. (1983). **The Conscious Use of Metaphor in Outward Bound**, Colorado Outward Bound School, Denver, Colorado.

Blocher, D. (1966). **Developmental Counseling**, The Ronald Press Co.

Bolton, Gavin (1979). **Towards a Theory of Drama in Education**, Longman.

Boud D., Keogh R. and Walker D. (1985). **Reflection: Turning Experience into Learning**, Kogan Page.

Dewey, John (1938). **Experience and Education**. Kappa Delta; then Collier, New York.

Kolb, David A. (1984). **Experience as the Source of Learning and Development**. Prentice Hall, Inc., Eaglewood Cliffs, New Jersey.

Miles, J. and Priest S. (eds). (1990). **Adventure Education**, Venture Publishing, Inc., 199 Cato Avenue, State College, PA 16801, U.S.A.

Manpower Service Commission (1984). **Residential Training in Y.T.S.: Youth Training Scheme Manual**, MSC, Sheffield.

Rogers, C. (1969). **Freedom to Learn: A view of what education might become**, C.E.Merrill, Columbus, Ohio.

Schofield, W. N. (1981). **Assessment of Personal and Social Development: a review of the literature**, DES, London.

Snell, R. (1988). **Learning at Work: creating the opportunities**, Local Government Training Board.

Thompson A. (1982). **Experience and Participation** (The Thompson Report on the Youth Service in England), H.M.S.O.

Warner Weil, S. and McGill, I. (eds). (1989). **Making Sense of Experiential Learning: diversity in theory and practice**, SRHE and Open University Press, Milton Keynes.

Wylie, T. (1987). **Counselling Young People: a practical introduction to informal counselling**, National Youth Bureau.

ADDRESSES FOR PUBLICATIONS AND INFORMATION

Adventure Education,
39, Brunswick Square, Penrith, CUMBRIA CA11 7LF

Association for Experiential Education,
Box 249-CU BOULDER, Colorado 80309, USA

British Association of Art Therapists,
c/o 13C, Northwood Road, London N6

British Association for Dramatherapists,
PO Box 98, Kirby Moorside, YORK YO6 6EX

Careers and Occupational Information Centre,
Room W1101, Moorfoot, SHEFFIELD S1 4PQ

Community Education Development Centre,
Brinton Road, COVENTRY CV2 4LF

Department for Education (publications),
Honeypot Lane, Canons Park, Stanmore, MIDDLESEX

Education for Capability,
Royal Society of Arts, 8, John Adam Street, LONDON WC2N 6EZ

Employment Department (publications) (formerly MSC)
Room W441, Moorfoot, SHEFFIELD S1 4PQ

Interlink,
(integration through arts for disabled and disadvantaged people)
142, The Strand, London WC2R 1HH

National Association for Outdoor Education,
5, The Wharf, Bridge Street BIRMINGHAM B1 2JS

National Association for Therapeutic Recreation,
Social Services, County Hall, West Bridgeford, NOTTS NG2 7QP

National Association for Values in Education and Training,
16, Butterley Drive, LOUGHBOROUGH LE11 OPX

National Youth Agency and Youth Work Press, (formerly NYB)
17-23, Albion Street, LEICESTER LE1 6GD

The Society for the Advancement of Games and Simulations
in Education and Training
Alan Cudworth, Dept. of Surveying, Nottingham Polytechnic,
NOTTINGHAM NG1 4BU

Youth Clubs UK (formerly NAYC),
Keswick House, 30, Peacock Lane, LEICESTER LE1 5NY

MAIN INDEX

Refer to page 29 for the index of methods by 'reviewing stage' (1-4) and by 'reviewing style' (active, creative, feedback, verbal, individual).

The 8 methods recommended for a 'basic toolkit' are listed in CAPITALS. The reasons for their selection are outlined on page 25.

ACKNOWLEDGEMENTS

I would like to acknowledge those from whom and with whom I have learned most about reviewing. For introducing me to reviewing: Bill Ryan, Chris Hillman, and my wife Lesley. For helping me to develop my reviewing skills: many of the staff who were working at the Brathay Hall Trust during the 1980's, especially Bridget Roberts, Steve Ripley, Bill Lloyd, Steve Crowther, Mike Cambray, and Nick Kell. For inspiring me to use drama and creative arts in reviewing: Richard Coaten, Bill Ryan, Chris Parry, Tony Rumgay, Christina MacDonald, Ali Temesy-Mackay, Dave Dodwell, Carla Billingham and the Gog Theatre Company. For demonstrating that young people of all abilities enjoy reviewing: Annie Cooper, Ali Crabb, Chloe Mossman, Jon Rigby, Chris Martucci, Phil Whitehurst, Liz Coldhurst, Wendy Maltinsky, and Phil Roycroft. For answering lots of questions about how they facilitate reviewing: Geoff Cox, Lorna Rylance, and Rudi Rengers. For helping me to think more clearly about experiential learning: Derrick Spragg, Bertie Everard, Bob Newman, Robin Snell, Julia Davies, Joyce Meade, Simon Priest, and Alan Mossman.

There are many other people who have kept my interest in reviewing alive: those who have asked me to provide training in reviewing skills; those who have participated creatively in my reviewing workshops; staff teams who have asked challenging questions about reviewing activities with young people; and the many young people who have shown that they are as good as (and often better than) adults at learning from experience, given half a chance.

I am grateful to those who have encouraged me to write about reviewing: Derrick Spragg, Chris Loynes, Bruce Britton, Bill Grieve, Jon Rigby, Phil Roycroft, Phil Maughan and Maralyn Lewis; to Joanna Buckley for the expert proof-reading; and to the organisations which have funded the production and publication of *Playback*:

The Special Projects Group of The Duke of Edinburgh's Award,
Endeavour Scotland,
The Trustee Savings Bank and
The Bank of Scotland.

THE PUBLISHERS

The Duke of Edinburgh's Award is a comprehensive programme of practical, cultural and adventurous activities for use by all agencies having a concern for the development of young people. The programme is flexible enough to meet the enthusiasms and aptitudes of young people of all abilities, whatever their background or culture, and however plentiful or limited their resources. The use of creative reviewing can ensure that young people gain the maximum educational benefit from their participation in the Scheme.

The Award gives opportunities for personal achievement, community and social involvement, adventure, and the discovery of new talents and interests. Since the criteria for gaining an Award are individual improvement and achievement, all young people, including those with special needs, can participate fully.

The Duke of Edinburgh's Award, Tel. 0753 810753
Gulliver House, Madeira Walk, Windsor, BERKSHIRE SL4 1EU

Endeavour Scotland is a registered Scottish Charity. The philosophy of valuing and inspiring human potential is fundamental to the work of both wings of Endeavour: the Training Wing provides personal, leadership and team development courses, mainly for commerce and industry; and the Community Development Wing works for young people experiencing difficulty, discrimination and disadvantage.

The reviewing of activities is a central feature of Endeavour Scotland's work, both in helping people to learn from experience, and in providing training or consultancy for those who wish to develop their reviewing skills.

Endeavour Scotland, Tel. 08775 292/3
The Boyd Centre, Dykehead, Port of Menteith, STIRLING FK8 3JY

DISTRIBUTION

Playback is distributed to the book trade by:

The Award Scheme Ltd.,
69, Dublin Street, Edinburgh EH3 6NS

BY THE SAME AUTHOR

Roger Greenaway's first handbook, **More Than Activities**, Save The Children Fund (1990), is about ways of using activity-based learning in work with young people (and is based on the work of the Advice project at Endeavour Scotland). The author has also produced articles and reports on active learning for the Group Relations Training Association (1983 & 1984); the Brathay Hall Trust and the Manpower Service Commission (1986); the I.T. Resources Centre (1988 & 1990); the National Youth Bureau (1991); the Association of Youth Work Trainers (1991); Endeavour Scotland and the BBC Children in Need Appeal (1992); and the Journal of Adventure Education and Outdoor Leadership (1992 & 1993). The author is currently seeking funding through Endeavour Scotland for producing a third handbook - about *evaluating* activity-based learning.

What they said about 'MORE THAN ACTIVITIES'

(continued from back cover)

'A lively handbook of practical information and ideas for anyone who works with young people.' *SCAN*

'Hundreds of gems of ideas, information, exercises, anecdotes and lots of questions which any good youth/youth social worker ought to be addressing.' *I.T. Resource Centre*

'Likely not only to make a major contribution to the growing success of educating through experience, but also to assist in the 'conversion' of many traditional practitioners on the way.' *John Cheesmond, Moray House College*

'A book which challenges us to examine our belief that taking part in the elements we offer is in itself sufficient to stimulate personal development.' *Scottish Journal of Physical Education*

'An imaginative practice manual full of good ideas, programmes, exercises and suggestions ... This manual stimulates those involved with youth to consider a whole range of options that have been tried and tested at the sharp end of practice.' *John Harding, Chief Probation Officer, Hampshire*

MORE THAN ACTIVITIES is available by post at £4.95 + 50p p&p from: Adventure Education, 39 Brunswick Square, Penrith, CUMBRIA CA11 7LF

MORE THAN ACTIVITIES, ISBN 1-870322-21-5, is supplied to the book trade by: CORDEE, 3a De Montfort Street, LEICESTER LE1 7HD